NEW CENTURY CHINESE WORKBOOK

I

新世纪汉语
练习册

第一册

萧惠媛　杨　颖　编
Emily Huang　Ying Petersen

北京语言大学出版社

（京）新登字 157 号

图书在版编目（CIP）数据

新世纪汉语练习册·第 1 册/萧惠媛，杨颖编．
－北京：北京语言大学出版社，2003
ISBN 7 - 5619 - 1269 - 2
Ⅰ．新…
Ⅱ．①萧… ②杨…
Ⅲ．对外汉语教学 - 习题
Ⅳ．H195.4 - 44
中国版本图书馆 CIP 数据核字（2003）第 106494 号

责任印制：乔学军
出版发行：北京语言大学出版社
社　　址：北京海淀区学院路 15 号　邮政编码 100083
网　　址：http://www.blcup.com
印　　刷：北京北林印刷厂
经　　销：全国新华书店
版　　次：2004 年 4 月第 1 版　2004 年 4 月第 1 次印刷
开　　本：889 毫米×1194 毫米　1/16　印张：19.5
字　　数：300 千字　印数：1 - 3000 册
书　　号：ISBN 7 - 5619 - 1269 - 2/H·03095
　　　　　2003 DW 0033
　　　　　04800

出版部电话：010 - 82303590
发行部电话：010 - 82303651　82303591
　　　传真：010 - 82303081
E-mail：fxb@blcu.edu.cn

如有印装质量问题·本社出版部负责调换

PREFACE

This workbook was compiled as the companion to the textbook *New Century Chinese* Book I. Since we are part of the textbook writing team as well as the instructors at one of the universities which have adopted the textbook, we have tried to reflect the characteristics of the textbook as much as we can, and explore the most efficient way for both readers and instructors to use the textbook easily.

The organization of the workbook, except for the preliminary section (*pinyin* system and Chinese character exercises), consists of the following elements:
1. Sentence pattern chart: Giving students an overview of all the grammatical points.
2. Character chart: Serving as a reference for students to preview and review all the new vocabulary.
3. Character writing sheet: Providing the stroke order as well as radical for each characte, and leaving room for students to practice *pinyin* and the English translation of individual words and to make phrases.
4. Pronunciation exercises: Distinguishing the sounds and practicing the *pinyin* spelling.
5. Listening comprehension exercises: Providing more listening exercises for each lesson.
6. Listening comprehension test: Allowing students to self-test their listening comprehension skills.
7. Character exercises: Reinforcing the memorization of characters through
    a) distinguishing similar sounds and characters, and
    b) identifying the radicals of characters.
8. Translation exercises: Practicing both vocabulary and grammar.
9. Writing exercises: By filling in the blanks in short passages, students can learn not only the writing of the words, but also the interpretation of the paragraphs related to the text.
10. Special topic exercises/readings/essays: Providing more comprehensive exercises on difficult topics.
11. Chapter exercises: Serving as a general review sheet for the whole chapter.

Through teaching the NCC Book I at the University of California in Irvine, we have been experimenting with various exercises to make this workbook more user-friendly. We would like to express our deepest gratitude to our colleagues Ruohmei Hsieh, Agnes Sun-Leah, Jessica Liu, Di Wu, and Jennifer Moldonado, who have helped us to test and to gather feedback from students on the material used in this book. Our special thanks go to Professor Xiaozhou Wu. His encouragement and suggestion have inspired us to finish this book. We welcome all suggestions from other readers and instructors.

> Emily Huang
> Department of East Asian Languages & Civilization
> Harvard University
>
> Ying Petersen
> Department of East Asian Languages & Literatures
> University of California, Irvine

CONTENTS

Preliminary ········· (1)

Pinyin System ········· (3)
Chinese Characters ········· (15)
 • A Brief Introduction to Chinese Characters ········· (17)
 • Important Sides or Radicals
  (Book One, Simplified Version) ········· (23)

NCC Book I ········· (35)

Step 1: Introduction & Greetings ········· (35)
Step 2: Time & Dates ········· (83)
Step 3: About Your Classmates ········· (131)
Step 4: Descriptions ········· (173)
Step 5: Classroom & Classes ········· (225)

Guided Composition: My Best Friend ········· (279)
Class & Self-Evaluation ········· (285)
Appendix: Tape scripts and Keys ········· (287)

Group:_____ Name:_____

Preliminary
Week 1: *Pinyin* System
Chinese Characters

Homework Assignment List:
Dictation score: _____ + _____ + _____ + _____ = _____
Homework score: _____ + _____ + _____ + _____ = _____

Date	NCC I Workbook	NCC I Textbook	Others

Comments: **Suggestions:**

PINYIN SYSTEM

Do You Know?

1. There are _400+_ basic syllables in the standard modern Chinese.

2. Most syllables of Chinese are made up of _initial_ and _final_.

3. There are _4_ basic tones in Chinese.

4. When a 3rd tone is followed by another 3rd tone, the former is pronunced as _second_ tone.

5. When "j" is combined with "ü", the compound word should be written as _ju_.

Pinyin Table

21 Initials:

1. Labials	b	p	m	f
2. Dentals	d	t	n	l
3. Velars	g	k	h	
4. Palatal	j	q	x	
5. Retroflex	zh	ch	sh	r
6. Alveolar	z	c	s	

15 Finals without Medials:

1. Single vowels (Medials)	i	u	ü	
2. Single vowels	a	o	e	
3. Diphthongs (w/medials)	ai	ei	ao	ou
4. Diphthongs (Nasal ending)	an	ang	en	eng
5. Diphthongs (w/retroflex)	er			

20 Finals with Medials:

1. Triphthongs Finals w/medial i	ia	ie	iao	iu
	ian	iang	in	ing
2. Triphthongs Finals w/medial u	ua	uai	uo	ui
	uan	uang	un	ong
3. Triphthongs Finals w/medial ü	üe	üan	ün	iong

Pinyin Spelling Rules

A: If there are no initials before the following finals, then you should

change	i	ia	ie	iao	iou	ian	in	iang	ing	iong	u
into	yi	ya	ye	yao	you	yan	yin	yang	ying	yong	wu

change	ua	uo	uai	uei	uan	uen	uang	ueng	ü	üe	üan	ün
into	wa	wo	wai	wei	wan	wen	wang	weng	yu	yue	yuan	yun

B: If j, q and x are followed by ü, you should

change	jü	qü	xü
into	ju	qu	xu

C: If there are initials before these finals, you should

change	n+iou	g+uei	l+uen
into	niu	gui	lun

D: n and l can be followed by both u and ü, therefore when n and l are followed by ü, then ü should remain ü.

Group:_____ Name:_____

Pinyin Spelling Rule Exercises

		With no initials	With initials			
1	i	yǐ	lǐ			
2	ia		l____			
3	ian		l____			
4	iang		l____			
5	iao		l____			
6	ie		l____			
7	in		l____			
8	ing		l____			
9	iong					x____
10	iou		l____			
11	u		h____			
12	ua		h____			
13	uai		h____			
14	uan		h____			
15	uang		h____			
16	uei		h____			
17	uen		h____			
18	ueng					
19	uo		h____			
20	ü		l____	j____	q____	x____
21	üan			j____	q____	x____
22	üe		l____	j____	q____	x____
23	ün			j____	q____	x____

7

Pinyin Exercises

Please listen to the recording/on-line and do the follwing exercises.

I. Tone recognition (1): Circle the ones with the tones that you hear.

	1st(-)	2nd(ˊ)	3rd(ˇ)	4th(ˋ)
1	ma	ma	ma	ma
2	di	di	di	di
3	tu	tu	tu	tu
4	liu	liu	liu	liu
5	gun	gun	gun	gun
6	ju	ju	ju	ju
7	zhi	zhi	zhi	zhi
8	song	song	song	song
9	chen	chen	chen	chen
10	ran	ran	ran	ran

Tone recognition (2): Circle the ones with the correct tones that you hear.

1	kàn jià	kān jiā
2	lǎo shī	láo shì
3	guān xīn	guàn xīn
4	piào liàng	piāo liǎng
5	rèn shi	rén shì

II. Initial recognition: Circle the ones with the initials that you hear.

1	ba	pa	fa
2	can	kan	gan
3	ne	de	ge
4	xiang	shang	jiang
5	jiáo	diao	xiao
6	qin	chin	jin
7	quan	kuan	guan
8	zhen	gen	chen
9	shui	zui	sui
10	rou	zhou	chou

III. Final recognition: Circle the ones with the finals that you hear.

1	xiu	xu
2	qian	qiang
3	shi	she
4	dou	duo
5	yuan	yan
6	ping	pin
7	mo	mu
8	nü	nu
9	you	yu
10	liu	lu

IV. Spelling rule (1): Circle the *pinyin* with the correct spelling.

1	jūn	juñ
2	ìng	yìng
3	qióng	qíong
4	niú	nióu
5	duì	duǐ
6	wǒ	uǒ
7	qù	qü
8	yáng	iáng
9	yuén	yún
10	pō	puō

Spelling rule (2): Mark the tones you hear on the correct positions.

1	jingyan
2	chunjiu
3	quanwei
4	bianle
5	shenglüe

Spelling rule (3): Write down the *pinyin* equivalents.

1	中国	中國	
2	山水	山水	
3	前程	前程	
4	佛光缘	佛光緣	
5	信口开河	信口開河	

Chinese Characters

Do You Know?

1. Chinese characters are believed to have originated about _3000_ years ago.
2. In 19_50_, Chinese government began to simplify the structure of some characters to make them easier to write.
3. Please decode the following early pictographic scripts:

						meaning
rì	⊙	⊖	⊟	日	日	sun
yuè	D	?	D	月	月	moon
shuǐ	〳	⺀	氺	水	水	water

15

A Brief Introduction to Chinese Characters

The age-old Chinese mythology always attributes the invention of Chinese characters to Cang Jie (仓颉/倉頡 Cāng Jié), the four-eyed historiographer of the Yellow Emperor (黄帝 Huáng Dì), who was a legendary ruler around the 26th century BC and was held as the highly respected ancestor of the Han people, but no one can firmly support the attribution with indubitable evidence. In spite of this apocryphal story, quite a few modern philologists and paleographers have ventured a popular conjecture that Cang Jie was probably a real historical figure during the reign of the Yellow Emperor, who might have been largely responsible for collecting, sorting out and systematizing Chinese characters which had already been collectively invented before him. It goes without saying that this will remain as a feasible speculation before more substantial evidence is found.

In light of the recorded historical documents, however, one can know for a certainty that as the writing vehicle of the Chinese language, Chinese characters have been in use for over 3 000 years. About this no one will have any doubt. In Chinese tradition, six categories (六书/六書 liùshū) are recognized in terms of the construction of Chinese characters. These six categories or methods of character construction are formally discussed and expounded in Xu Shen's (许慎/許慎 ca. 58-147AD) work Analysis and Explanation of Characters (说文解字/說文解字 Shuō Wén Jiě Zì), known to be the first Chinese dictionary ever compiled.

The pictographic method, which is employed to draw an object's shape in a rough and simple manner, is believed to be the earliest way to create characters. The characters created in this way are called "pictographs" (象形字 xiàngxíngzì). Some of the typical pictographs are: 山 shān (mountain), 日 rì (sun), 月 yuè (moon), 人 rén (person), 木 mù (tree) and 口 kǒu (mouth). But there are not many pictographs in the Chinese writing system, since this method is rather limited. The second category of characters are called "self-explanatory ideographs" (指事 zhǐshì). Symbols and pictographs are both used in the method to indicate abstract meanings. Here are some examples: 一 yī (one), 二 èr (two), 上 shàng (up), 下 xià (down), 本 běn (root), 刃 rèn (blade). The number of the self-explanatory ideographs are also very limited. The associative method, which combines two or more ideographic symbols to form a new character, is used to create the so-called associative compound ideographs (会意字/會意字 huìyìzì), among which (林 lín, wood), (森 sēn, forest), (见/見 jiàn, see), (休 xiū, rest), and (信 xìn, trust) are good examples.

Although the number of the associative compound ideographs is bigger than either of the first two categories, it can hardly be compared to that of the fourth category, whose characters constitute at least 80 percent of the total number of all the existing Chinese characters. The characters pertaining to the fourth category are called pictophonetic compound characters (形声字/形聲字 xíngshēngzì). In this method, typically, a phonetic component (声旁/聲旁 shēngpáng) which indicates the pronunciation of the character in question and a signific radical (形旁 xíngpáng) which denotes its meaning are combined to form a new character. With this method one can create quite a few new characters that all sound the same but with different meanings. For example, all these characters 湖(lake), 糊(paste), 蝴(butterfly), 葫(gourd), 猢(monkey), 鹕/鶘(pelican) are pronounced as (胡 hú), which serves as their mutual phonetic component, but they mean different things because of their different signific radicals: 氵(water), 米(rice), 虫(insect), 艹(plant), 犭(animal), and 鸟/鳥 (bird). Judging from this feature, many Chinese characters may, just like any alphabetical languages, provide some sort of pronunciations for the reader who has mastered enough basic components and radicals. In fact, this is only partially true. One of the main reasons is that most of the phonetic components have already lost their ability to accurately indicate pronunciations, since there have been constant changes and sometimes great mutations in the pronunciations of the language over the long years of currency. Moreover, in terms of their meanings, even some of the signific radicals which originally only indicated the general relation to the meanings of individual characters have also undergone great changes over the long years of currency. For these main reasons, some philologists even try to argue that sometimes it is more detrimental to the learning process of this type of characters than it is helpful to it. However, no one can totally deny the usefulness of the knowledge about the phonetic components and the signific radicals in the recognition and writing of the pictophonetic characters.

In comparison with the first four methods of character construction, the last two methods are rather insignificant, for they merely expand the range of use of characters in a moderate way, therefore only a small number of characters belong to these two categories. Synonymous characters (转注字/轉註字 zhuǎnzhùzì) refer to those characters whose sounds, meanings and written forms have undergone some sort of modification. For example, (爸 bà, dad) is derived from (父 fù, father), (船 chuán, ship) derived from (舟 zhōu, boat), and (顶/頂 dǐng, peak) derived from (颠/顛 diān, summit). The characters belonging to the sixth method are called phonetic loan characters (假借字 jiǎjièzì). This method is employed when an extant homophonous character is borrowed to indicate another word that lacks a written form. For example, the original meaning of the extant character "來 lái" refers to some kind of wheat, but later it is borrowed to indicate the word lacking a written form, which now takes the form of "来/來", meaning "to come".

As one of the world's oldest written language, Chinese has undergone, just like any other living languages, continuous evolution and sometimes even drastic changes since its invention. In terms of the general trend directing the evolution of the forms of the Chinese characters, they have been slowly but steadily transformed from complexity to simplicity, from unsystematization to standardization, and from pictographic or ideographic writing to pictographic writing.

To this day, oracle bone inscriptions (甲骨文 jiǎgǔwén) still remain the oldest Chinese characters ever found. The inscriptions, which were found accidentally in 1899, refer to divinatory texts in the form of Chinese characters inscribed on tortoise carapaces and mammal bones in the Shang Dynasty (1711—1066 BC). Among the 4 500 individual characters found and identified, about 1 000 are believed to have been correctly deciphered. In terms of their forms, strokes, stroke orders and radicals, the oracle bone inscriptions are hardly stable and standardized yet, although they clearly demonstrate that they have already broken away from the primitive patterns and a well-organized writing system is being established.

During the late Shang Dynasty and throughout the Zhou Dynasty (1066—256 BC), the style of bronze inscriptions—characters cast or engraved on bronzewares (mainly bronze bells, tripods, sacrificial vessels and weapons)—is current. Although bronze inscriptions bear striking similarities to their predecessors—oracle bone inscriptions, they are also very close in form to their immediate descendants—the seal script (篆书/篆書 zhuànshū). Among the 3 000 individual characters collated, about 2 000 can be deciphered. Bronze inscription characters are more symmetrical in form and regular in size, and their format is more stable, but they still remain unstandardized.

The unification of China by the first emperor of the Qin Dynasty (221—206 BC) also gives rise to the official promulgation of the small seal script (小篆 xiǎozhuàn) as the standard form of writing for the entire country. Small seal characters, which are a simplification of great seal script (大篆 dàzhuàn) used before the country's unification, bear similarities to bronze script, but they are less pictographic and more pictophonetic, and much neater in structure. Moreover, they have begun to establish the square-shape characteristic of later characters.

From the end of the Qin Dynasty, a new style of writing called official script (隶书/隸書 lìshū), which is simplified from small seal script, has been put to use. It continues to be current as the formal written language in the Han Dynasty (206 BC—220 AD) and even lasts to the Three Kingdoms Period (220—280 AD). In its earlier version, official script still bears certain characteristics of small seal script, but in its later version, level, straight and broken strokes are added, and the complicated strokes and radicals simplified—all these features have transformed the characters with their originally pictographic nature into pure written symbols of speech. Marking the completion of the transition from the ancient scripts to the modern scripts, official script has been justifiably considered as the turning point in the evolution history of Chinese characters.

Directly derived from official script, regular script (楷书/楷書 kǎishū) begins to replace the former as the principal style of Chinese characters at the end of the Han Dynasty, and it has been in continuous use up to this day. With the further finalized standardization and regularization, regular script has been regarded as the standard of Chinese character structure since then. Being characterized by their straight and level lines and their well-balanced square shape, Chinese characters are also known as the so-called square characters (方块字 fāngkuàizì).

Along the other line of the evolution of Chinese characters, cursive script (草书/草書 cǎoshū), another style of writing, also appears. The earliest form of this style known as cursive seal script (章草 zhāngcǎo) is also derived from official script at the beginning of the Han Dynasty. Its purpose is to cursively write down characters as quickly as possible in its daily uses. Toward the end of the Han Dynasty, a new type of cursive writing called contemporary cursive script (今草 jīncǎo) emerges. It completely breaks away from its predecessors in form. With strokes linked closely and even characters connected in a cursive fashion, the style becomes more unorthodox and hard to read. Later, in the Tang Dynasty (618—907 AD), it evolves into another very different style called crazy cursive script (狂草 kuángcǎo), whose strokes flow unbrokenly and irregularly, and often willfully omitted, thus making the characters hardly legible.

Somewhere between the loose and free-wheeling cursive script and the formal and rigid regular script, there appears a new style of writing called running script (行书/行書 xíngshū). Mainly derived from regular script and partially from cursive script, it bears the nice features of both its predecessors. While maintaining the basic form of regular script which makes the characters very legible, this style allows at the same time some linkage of strokes which do not run so wildly as those of cursive script, and therefore it enables one to write much faster than one does regular script, and it is also much easier to read than cursive script. As a result, it has been widely accepted as the most practical style, which is used in daily writing activities by hand like taking notes and writing letters. Here it should be pointed out that understandably, for practical and artistic purposes, there exist some minor differences between the hand-written characters of running script and the printed characters of regular script (there are mainly four styles currently used in printing shops: the Old Song Style (老宋体/老宋體 lǎosòngtǐ), the imitative Song Style (仿宋体/仿宋體 fǎngsòngtǐ), the Grand Song Style (大宋体/大宋體 dàsòngtǐ[i. e. the regular script]), and the Black Bold Style (黑体字/黑體字 hēitǐzì)), just like those between the hand-written letters and the printed ones in the English language.

After the founding of the People's Republic of China in 1949, there have been four efforts by the government, in 1950, 1956, 1964, and 1977 respectively, to promote the simplification of Chinese characters in the mainland China. All the efforts, except the last one, have resulted in some kind of success. The first three efforts have brought about the simplification of over 2000 characters. The characters used in the simplified version of the present textbook are those of the first three efforts, whereas the characters used in the traditional version are those that have been in use since the end of the Han Dynasty, which are still currently used in Taiwan, Hong Kong and among the overseas Chinese communities.

According to The Great Chinese Dictionary (汉语大字典/漢語大字典 Hànyǔ Dà Zìdiǎn) published in 1986, the largest Chinese dictionary ever complied, there are at least 56,000 characters in existence, and only a small number of them (less than one tenths) are in daily use. Although that small number is still big enough to intimidate any weak-minded novice learner of Chinese, the structure of the characters is by no means complicated and intricate. Basically, Chinese characters can be divided into two categories: the single-component characters (独体字/獨體字 dútǐzì), such as 山, 人, 日, 月, 木, and the compound characters (合体字/合體字 hétǐzì), such as 明, 好, 你, 休. The former category, which constitutes only a very small number of the total characters, is regarded as an integral unit that cannot be dissected, whereas the latter, which constitutes the majority of the total characters, is usually made up of two or more basic components or sides (偏旁 piānpáng), many of which are conventionally used as the radicals (部首 bùshǒu) in the Chinese dictionaries that use the radical method to classify characters. The knowledge of these radicals will not only help one to memorize characters better and faster, but also enable one to look up characters and words in a Chinese dictionary that uses the radicals to classify characters. The important sides or radicals will be introduced and explained one by one when they appear for the first time in the following chapters of the present character workbook.

In terms of the forms of structure, the compound characters can be roughly divided into three major types: the left-right structure, the top-bottom structure, and the enclosing or half-enclosing structure, such as 妈/媽, 朋, 字, 男, 国/國 and 同 for each type, respectively. In addition, there are some other minor forms of structure of compound characters, but most of them are just their variants or combination of these three major types.

Chinese characters can be further decomposed into various lines or dots called "strokes", the smallest elements in the character structure. The 30-odd strokes may be boiled down to only 8 basic strokes:

笔画/筆畫 bǐhuà Strokes	名称/名稱 míngchēng Stroke Names	例字 lìzì Examples
丶	点/點 diǎn dot	文、六

笔画/筆畫 bǐhuà Strokes	名称/名稱 míngchēng Stroke Names	例字 lìzì Examples
一	横 héng horizontal stroke	丁、三
丨	竖/豎 shù vertical stroke	中、十
丿	撇 piě left-falling stroke	人、八
丶	捺 nà right-falling stroke	天、大
╱	提 tí rising stroke	我、打
㇖ 亅 乚	勾 gōu hook	客、你、找、心、見
𠃍 ㄴ	折 zhé turning stroke	口、山

It should be noted here that it is very important for a beginner of Chinese to learn how to count the number of strokes in a character, because knowing the exact number of strokes will enable him or her to efficiently look up a character in a dictionary which classifies characters according to the number of strokes.

For both practical and aesthetic purposes, the stroke order (笔顺/筆順 bǐ shùn) is also of vital importance to the beginner when he or she produces the strokes in writing characters. Conventionally, certain rules should be observed when one is engaged in writing them. In the following table, eight general rules for the stroke order and some typical examples are provided:

规则/規則 guīzé Rules	例字 lìzì Examples	笔画/筆畫 bǐhuà Stroke Order
先横后竖/先橫後豎 xiān héng hòu shù Horizontal stroke before vertical stroke	十	一十
先撇后捺/先撇後捺 xiān piě hòu nà Left-falling stroke before right-falling stroke	人	丿人
从上到下/從上到下 cóng shàng dào xià From top to bottom	三	一 二 三
从左到右/從左到右 cóng zuǒ dào yòu From left to right	你	亻你
从外到里/從外到裡 cóng wài dào lǐ From outside to inside	月	丿 冂 月

规则/規則 guīzé Rules	例字 lìzì Examples	笔画/筆畫 bǐhuà Stroke Order
先外后里再封口/先外後裡再封口 xiān wài hòu lǐ zài fēng kǒu From outside to inside before sealing stroke	困	冂 困 困
先中间后两边/先中間後兩邊 xiān zhōng jiān hòu liǎng biān Middle before left side & right side	小	亅 小 小

Of course, these are just some important general rules, and one should always exercise flexibly when applying them in writing characters. To avoid writing characters in an incorrect order, we would like to advice the user of the present workbook to closely follow the order of the characters provided when he or she first learns to write.

Finally, a word of encouragement to the beginners of Chinese characters. It almost goes without saying that Chinese characters are, as compared with the alphabetical languages, much harder to learn, yet they are not insurmountable. Nothing is hard in this world if one sets one's heart on it. It is our strong belief that Chinese characters can be learned and mastered through sustained efforts and constant practices. As the saying goes, "no gains without pains", one's painstaking labor will be handsomely rewarded when one has mastered the writing system of the Chinese language, which is used by 1.3 billion people in this world.

Important Sides or Radicals
(Book One, Simplified Version)

1) "辶" was derived from the ancient character "辵", meaning "walking". The characters with this radical are usually related to walking or moving. Examples: 这, 进 (jìn, to enter), 达 (dá, to arrive) and 道 (dào, way).

2) "亻" is the variant form of the formal character "人", which resembles the drawing of a human being or person. Therefore the characters with this radical are usually related to people. Examples: 位, 你 (nǐ, you), 们 (mén, *a suffix which indicates the plural form of people*) and 他 (tā, he).

3) "女" means "female", so the characters with it are usually related to women. Examples: 好 (a woman holding a child "子" in her arms, symbolizing goodness or blessing), 姓 (xìng, surname), 姐 (jiě, elder sister), and 她 (tā, she).

4) "心" is a pictograph which resembles a person's heart. Since ancient people believed that they thought with their hearts, so the characters with this radical are usually related to thinking and psychological activities. Examples: 您, 意思 (yìsi, meaning) and 想 (xiǎng, to think).

5) "戈" is a pictograph whose original form resembled an ancient weapon similar to a spear, so the characters with it are usually related to fighting or war. Examples: 我 (originally it referred to a weapon with a long shaft and three sharp points, and later it was loaned to mean "I"), 找 (zhǎo, to look for) and 战 (zhàn, to fight).

6) "人" means "human being", so the characters with it are usually related to people. Examples: 介, 个 (gè, *a measure word for people and places*) and 从 (cóng, from, follow).

7) "纟" is the variant form of "絲" (sī), originally meaning "intertwined silk". Some characters are still associated with its original meaning. Examples: 绍, 线 (xiàn, thread), and 绸 (chóu, satin).

8) "口" is a pictograph which resembles a person's mouth, therefore the characters with it are usually related to mouth. Examples: 叫 (jiào, to call), 吗 (ma, *a question particle*), 问 (wèn, to ask), 号 (hào, number, to cry) and 呢 (ne, *a modal particle*).

9) "月" was derived from four origins: Two clusters of cowries, moon, flesh and boat. Characters like 朋 (péng, friend) belongs to the first source; characters like 明 (míng, bright) and 星期 (xīngqī, week) to the second; characters like 腿 (tuǐ, leg), 脚 (jiǎo, foot), 腰 (yāo, waist) and 肚 (dù, stomach) to the third; and finally characters like 服 (fú, clothes) and 前 (qián, front) to the fourth.

10) "又" is a simplified symbol which resembles a person's right hand. Therefore the characters with this radical are usually related to hand. Examples: 友 (yǒu, friend [its original form signified a left hand and a right hand, hence a friend]), 对 (duì, correct, right) and 双 (shuāng, pair).

11) "讠" was the variant form of the character "言", meaning "speech", therefore the characters with this radical are usually related to language. Examples：请, 语（yǔ, language）, 说（shuō, to speak）, 谁（shéi, who）, 认识（rèn shi, to know）, 谢（xiè, to thank）and 课（kè, lesson）.

12) "门" is the simplified form of the pictographic character "門", symbolizing a door or gate. Examples：问, 们, 闷（mèn, bored）and 间（jiān, room）.

13) "夕", which was derived from the formal character "月"（yuè, moon）, literally means "dusk", but now it is simply used as a radial to classify characters in dictionaries. Examples：名, 多（duō, many）and 岁（suì, age）.

14) "宀" is a radical whose original form resembled the roof of a house, so the characters with it are usually related to home or living quarters. Examples：字, 家（jiā, home）, 安（ān, peace）, 宿（sù, dormitory）and 客（kè, guest）.

15) "贝" is a simplified form of the pictographic character "貝", which means "cowry" or "shellfish." Sea shells were used as currency in ancient times, so this radical usually suggests "wealth", "expensiveness" or "nobleness". Examples：贵（guì, expensive）, 财（cái, wealth）and 贫（pín, poor）.

16) "白" was originally the symbol of a burning candle, which suggests "bright" or "clear". Later it was extended to mean "white", to whose meaning some characters are still related. Examples：的, 百（bǎi, hundred）, 皇（huáng, emperor）, and 皎（jiǎo, white）.

17) "田" is a pictograph which symbolizes "cultivated land", therefore the characters with it are usually related to fields. Examples：男（nán, man）, 思（sī, think）and 留（liú, keep）.

18) "氵" is the variant form of the formal character 水（shuǐ）, which originally meant "stream", so the characters with this radical are closely related to water. Examples：汉, 海（hǎi, sea）, 河（hé, river）and 游泳（yóuyǒng, swim）.

19) "阝"（on the left of the character）was derived from the character "阜（fù）", meaning "mound". The characters with this radical are usually associated with hills or mountains. Examples：陈, 阳（yáng, sun）and 院（yuàn, yard）.

20) "日" is a pictograph which symbolizes "the sun". Later it was extended to indicate "day" or "time". Examples：早（zǎo, early）, 晚（wǎn, late）, 明（míng, bright）and 阳（yáng, the sun）.

21) "彳" originally meant "walking slowly", so the characters with it are usually related to movement. Examples：很, 行（xíng, walk）and 往（wǎng, go）.

22) "阝"（on the right of the character）was derived from the formal character "邑", which means "town" or "city". The character "都" is also pronounced as "dū", which means "capital" or "metropolis". Therefore the characters with this radical are usually related to cities or towns. Examples：都（dū, capital or city）, 那, 邦（bāng, state）and 邻（lín, neighbor）.

23) "忄"（*vertical heart*）is the variant form of the formal character "心"（xīn, heart）, so the char-

24

acters with it are usually related to thoughts and psychological activities. Examples: 忙, 慢 (màn, slow) and 快 (kuài, fast).

24) "土" is a pictograph whose original form resembled a dust heap, and later it was extended to mean "soil". Therefore the characters with this radical are usually related to earth or ground. Examples: 坐 (zuò, to sit), 在 (zài, in or on) and 地 (dì, land).

25) "⺮" is the variant form of the formal character 竹 (zhú), which means "bamboo", therefore the characters with it are usually related to bamboo. Examples: 第, 笔 (bǐ, pen), 笛 (dí, flute) and 等 (děng, wait).

26) "小" is a pictograph whose original form resembled three grains of sand, symbolizing "small" or "tiny". Examples: 少 (shǎo, few), 尘 (chén, dust) and 尖 (jiān, sharp).

27) "灬" was derived from the formal character "火" (huǒ), meaning "fire", so the characters with it are usually related to fire or heat. Examples: 点, 热 (rè, hot) and 煮 (zhǔ, to cook).

28) "钅" is the simplified form of the formal character "金" (jīn), which means "gold" or "metal". Therefore, the characters with this radical are often associated with metal. Examples: 钟 (zhōng, clock), 银 (yín, silver), 铁 (tiě, iron) and 钢 (gāng, steel).

29) "刂" is the variant form of the formal character "刀" (dāo), meaning "knife", so the characters with it are usually associated with cutting or carving. Examples: 刻 (kè, to cut), 分 (fēn, to divide), 到 (dào, to arrive), 刷 (shuā, to brush), 别 (bié, to separate) and 利 (lì, sharp).

30) "工" is a pictograph whose original form resembled a wood tamper, and was later extended to mean "work" or "worker". Some characters with it are still remotely associated with its original meaning. Examples: 差, 功 (gōng, effort, work) and 攻 (gōng, to attack).

31) "走" was derived from the drawing of a walking man, signifying "to run" or "to go", so the characters with it are usually related to going or walking. Examples: 起, 赴 (fù, to go) and 越 (yuè, to pass).

32) "广" originally meant a building whose front did not have a wall, so the characters with it are usually associated with a building. Examples: 床, 店 (diàn, shop) and 库 (kù, warehouse).

33) "饣" is simplified from the formal character "食" (shí), meaning "eating" or "food", so the characters with it are usually related to dining or meals. Examples: 饭 (fàn, meal), 饭馆 (fànguǎn, restaurant) and 饮 (yǐn, to drink).

34) "目" is a pictograph which symbolizes a person's eye, therefore the characters with it are usually related to one's eyes or vision. Examples: 睡 (shuì, to sleep), 眼睛 (yǎnjing, eye) and 见 [simplified from 見] (jiàn, to see).

35) "其" originally meant "dustpan". Now it is simply used to classify characters in dictionaries. Examples: 期 (qī, term), 斯 (sī, this) and 欺 (qī, to deceive).

36)"木" means "tree" or "wood", so the characters with it are usually related to a tree or wooden object. Examples：样 (yàng, shape),早 (zǎo, morning [when the sun rises above the trees]),床 (chuáng, bed), 桌 (zhuō, table),椅 (yǐ, chair),板 (bǎn, plank),本 (běn, root) and 李 (lǐ, plum).

37)"巾" is a pictograph whose original form resembled a towel or scarf, so the characters with it are usually related to cloth. Examples：常,帽 (mào, hat or cap),布 (bù, cloth) and 帕 (pà, handkerchief).

38)"冫" originally meant "ice", so the characters with it are usually associated with coldness. Examples：冷 (lěng, cold),冰 (bīng, ice) and 凉 (liáng, cool).

39)"冂" is the variant form of the formal character "同" (tóng), which originally meant "all with one voice", and later it was extended to mean "common" or "same". There are only a few characters that employ this radical. Examples：同 and 冈 (gāng, hillock).

40)"子" is a pictograph whose original form resembled an infant or baby, so the characters with it are usually related to children. Examples：学 (simplified from 學, symbolizing a child learning to count sticks with his hands in a house),孩子 (háizi, child),孙 (sūn, grandchild) and 孕 (yùn, pregnant).

41)"囗" is usually related to boundary or circumambiency. Examples：国 (guó, country),围 (wéi, to enclose),回 (huí, to return),图 (tú, picture) and 园 (yuán, yard).

42)"豕" is a pictograph whose original form resembled a boar, so the characters with it are usually related to animals. Examples：家,象 (xiàng, elephant) and 豬 (or its simplified form 猪 zhū, pig).

43)"羊" is a pictograph which resembles a sheep or goat with its horns. Therefore the characters with it are associated with sheep. Examples：美 (měi, beautiful [originally it meant a person with a goat-like costume on top]),羔 (gāo, lamb) and 群 (qún, flock).

44)"艹" was derived from the formal character "草" (cǎo), meaning "grass" or "plant". Therefore the characters with this radical are usually associated with plants. Examples：英 (yīng, blossom), 蓝 (lán, indigo blue) and 花 (huā, flower).

45)"山" is a pictograph which resembles a mountain or hill, so the characters with it are usually related to mountains. Examples：岁,山 (shān, mountain),岭 (lǐng, ridge) and 峰 (fēng, peak).

46)"攵" is a pictograph whose original form resembled a hand holding a pointer to teach a child a lesson, so the characters with it are usually related to education and authority. Examples：数,教 (jiāo, to teach),政 (zhèng, politics) and 牧 (mù, to herd).

47)"父" was derived from a symbol that resembled a hand holding a stone ax, signifying a laboring man. Later it was extended to mean "father", so the characters with this radical are usually related to male seniors of a family. Examples：爸,父 (fù, father),爹 (diē, dad) and 爷 (yé, grandpa).

48)"王" was derived from the formal character "玉" (yù), which means "jade", so the characters with it are usually related to precious stones. Examples：现,玛瑙 (mǎnǎo, agate) and 玩 (wán, curio).

49) "舌" is a pictograph whose original form resembled a person's tongue, so the characters with it are either phonetically or semantically related to language. Examples: 舌 (shé, tongue), 话 (huà, speech or word) and 甜 (tián, sweet).

50) "石" originally meant "chime-stone", and later it was extended to indicate "stone" or "rock", so the characters with it are usually related to stone or ore. Examples: 码, 矿 (kuàng, mine) and 砂 (shā, sand).

51) "衤" is the variant form of the pictographic character "衣" (yī), which was derived from the picture of an ancient jacket. Therefore the characters with it are usually related to garments. Examples: 衬衫 (chèn shān, shirt), 裤 (kù, pants), 裙 (qún, skirt) and 袜 (wà, sock).

52) "穴" is a pictograph which symbolizes a cave or grotto, so the characters with it are usually related to holes or caverns. Examples: 穿 (chuān, to penetrate, to wear), 空 (kōng, empty) and 窗 (chuāng, window).

53) "革" is a pictograph whose original form resembled a spread-out hide of a flayed animal, so the characters with it are usually related to leather or hide. 鞋 (xié, shoes), 靴 (xuē, boot) and 靶 (bǎ, target).

54) "米" means "uncooked rice", so the characters with it are usually related to food. Examples: 粗, 糖 (táng, sugar), 粉 (fěn, noodles) and 糕 (gāo, cake).

55) "矢" is a pictograph whose original form resembled an arrow with its arrowhead and nock. The characters that use this radical include 短 (duǎn, short), 矮 (ǎi, short) and 知 (zhī, to know).

56) "疒" was derived from the character "病" (bìng), meaning "to be sick" or "illness". So the characters with this radical are usually related to diseases or sicknesses. Examples: 疼 (téng, pain), 瘦 (shòu, skinny), 痛 (tòng, ache) and 疾病 (jíbìng, disease).

57) "牛" is a pictograph whose original form resembled an ox, so the characters with it are usually related to cattle. Examples: 特 (tè, special, ox [original meaning]), 物 (wù, thing) and 牧 (mù, to herd).

58) "禾" is a pictograph whose original form resembled a ripe rice plant, so the characters with it are usually associated with cereal plants. Examples: 和, 香 (xiāng, fragrant), 种 (zhòng, to plant) and 秋 (qiū, autumn).

59) "扌" is the variant of the formal pictographic character "手" (shǒu), whose original form resembled a man's hand, so the characters with it are usually related to hand. Examples: 把 (bǎ, handle, *a measure word for things with a handle*), 授 (shòu, to give, to confer), 看 (kàn, to look, to see, to read [covering the eye with a hand to see better]), 拉 (lā, to pull) and 打 (dǎ, to beat).

60) "户" is a pictograph whose original form resembled a leaf of a door, and later it was extended to indicate "household" or "family", so the characters with it are usually related to home or house. Examples: 扇 (shàn, fan, *a measure word for things that look like the shape of a fan*), 房 (fáng, house) and 所 (suǒ, abode).

61) "斤" is a pictograph which resembled a stone ax, and later it was extended to mean "catty"—a unit of weight. Therefore the characters with it are usually related to cutting or weight. Examples: 新 (xīn, new, firewood [original meaning]), 斧 (fǔ, ax) and 断 (duàn, to break).

62) "弓" is a pictograph which resembles a bow, so the characters with it are usually associated with stretching and extension. Examples: 张 (zhāng, *a measure word*, to open or stretch [original meaning]), 弹 (tán, to pluck, to play) and 弦 (xián, string).

63) "厂" originally meant "living quarter under the cliff", so the characters with it are usually associated with houses. Examples: 历, 厅 (tīng, hall), 厨 (chú, kitchen) and 厕 (cè, rest room).

64) "母" is a pictograph whose original form resembled a mother kneeling down with her breasts exposed, ready to feed her baby. Therefore the characters with it are usually related to mother or motherhood. Examples: 每, 母 (mǔ, mother) and 毋 (wù, not [archaic]).

65) "页" is a pictograph whose original form resembled a head, so the characters with it are usually linked with one's head or face. 题, 顶 (dǐng, top), 领 (lǐng, collar) and 须 (xū, mustache).

66) "⻊" is the variant form of "足" (zú), meaning "foot", so the characters with it are usually related to foot or walking. Examples: 跟 (gēn, heel), 路 (lù, road) and 踢 (tī, to kick).

67) "隹" is a pictograph whose original form resembled a pheasant, so the characters with it are either phonetically or semantically related poultry. Examples: 难, 谁 (shéi/shuí, who), 雀 (què, bird) and 雁 (yàn, wild goose).

68) "礻" is the variant form of the formal character "示" (shì), which probably meant "a god of land" in ancient times. Therefore the characters with this radical are usually related to gods or rituals. Examples: 福 (fú, good fortune), 礼 (lǐ, rite), 祝 (zhù, to wish) and 神 (shén, god).

69) "冖" was probably derived from the formal character "幂" (mì), which originally meant "cloth cover". Now it is simply used as a radical to classify characters in dictionaries. Examples: 写 (xiě, to write), 军 (jūn, military, army) and 农 (nóng, agriculture, peasant).

70) "力" originally meant "a ploughing instrument", and later it was extended to indicate "strength". Examples: 助 (zhù, to help), 男 (nán, male, man) and 劳动 (láodòng, labor).

Selected Radicals of Chinese Characters

Radicals	Meanings	Examples	Your Input
一	one	上下不三且	
人/亻	man	今休他你作	
冫	ice	冷冰冬	
刀/刂	knife	刻到刮判剩分	
力	strength	加功岁	
口	mouth	吃喝吸唱名同	
囗	enclosure	因四回囚	
土	earth	城地址坐在塞	
大	great	太天夫失奇	
女	female	姓好姑娘姐妹	
子	child/son	孩字孔	
宀	roof	字家室客宿定完	
巾	napkin	帽常希市	
广	shelter	床座店康	
彳	left step	行很待得	
氵	water	酒波河洗游泳	
心/忄	heart	思想忙懂快慢	
手/扌	hand	拿打把接找拔指	
日	sun, day	早晚星明昨春是	
月	moon	有望朋服期	
木	wood, tree	本李果杯桌椅	
火/灬	fire	炒然黑	
王	jade	玩班球玲	
田	field	男留界	
疒	sick	病瘦疤	
目	eye	看睡	
礻	reveal	社祝	
竹	bamboo	笑笨算第答筷	

Radicals	Meanings	Examples	Your Input
米	rice	精糖糟粥	
纟 / 糹	silk	给绍结纸红 / 給紹結紙紅	
老	old	老考	
耳	ear	取聊	
月（肉）	flesh	肚能腿胞	
艹	grass, herb	花草茶菜茅苞	
衤	clothes	裙衫被袍裹	
讠 / 言	word	请话语说诉谢课 / 請話語說訴謝課	
贝 / 貝	shell	贵财负责 / 貴財負責	
走	to walk	起越	
足	foot	跑跪跟路跳踢	
车 / 車	cart	轻辆输载轰 / 輕輛輸載轟	
辶	to run & stop	追送迎	
阝	city	都那	
酉	wine	酒酪	
钅 / 金	gold, metal	钱银锻钓错 / 錢銀鍛釣錯	
门 / 門	door	问闻间阅 / 問聞間閱	
阝	mound	院阳陪	
雨	rain	雨雪雷	
饣 / 食	to eat	饭饿饱饺馆餐 / 飯餓飽餃館餐	

Exercises on Chinese Characters

Ⅰ. Stroke Type Recognition:
Circle the stroke types identified in the shaded column of the following characters.

Types of stroke	Examples	Characters
Horizontal stroke	王	不 正 干
Vertical stroke	上	中 丰 生
Left stroke	人	生 刀 大
Right stroke	入	衣 近 木
Dot	心	冰 黑 我
Hook	己	狗 戈 小
Turning stroke	日	又 九 句
Rising stroke	比	打 求 物

Ⅱ. Stroke Order Recognition:
Circle the character(s) which begin(s) with the same stroke as the one in the shaded column.

生	不	我	皮	方
是	作	同	用	因
的	月	坐	字	普
小	水	中	半	川

Ⅲ. Stroke Numbers:

介		水		然	
出		弟		客	
良		帽		孩	

Group:_____ Name:_____

New Century Chinese Book I
Step 1: Introduction & Greetings

Homework Assignment List:
Dictation score: _____+_____+_____+_____ = _____
Homework score: _____+_____+_____+_____ = _____

Date	NCC I Workbook	NCC I Textbook	Others

Comments: **Suggestions:**

NCC Step 1 Summary of the Sentence Patterns

Items	Patterns	Sample Sentences
1	吗	你好吗？ 你是王大贵吗？
2	呢	我很好，你呢？ 我不是老师，你呢？
3	Nominal predicate	您贵姓？
4	Adj. as the predicate	你好！ 我很忙。
5	Verb as the predicate	他姓王，他叫大来。 他不是老师。 我介绍一下儿。
6	What（什么）	你叫什么名字？
7	Whom（谁） Who（谁）	那是谁？ 谁认识他？
8	也（also） 都（all）	我很忙，他也很忙。 他们也都很忙。

NCC Step 1 Summary of the Sentence Patterns

Items	Patterns	Sample Sentences
1	嗎	你好嗎？ 你是王大貴嗎？
2	呢	我很好，你呢？ 我不是老師，你呢？
3	Nominal predicate	您貴姓？
4	Adj. as the predicate	你好！ 我很忙。
5	Verb as the predicate	他姓王，他叫大來。 他不是老師。 我介紹一下兒。
6	What（甚麼）	你叫甚麼名字？
7	Whom（誰） Who（誰）	那是誰？ 誰認識他？
8	也（also） 都（all）	我很忙，他也很忙。 他們也都很忙。

NCC Step 1 Characters

Required Characters

	A	B	C	D	E	F	G	H	I	J
1	这這	位	是	老	师師	你	们們	好	您	我
2	来來	介	绍紹	下	儿兒	姓	叫	小	朋	友
3	什甚	么麼	他	她	请請	问問	先	生	名	字
4	姐	贵貴	吗嗎	的	女	男	汉漢	语語	谁誰	不
5	认認	识識	早	晚	上	再	见見	呢	也	很
6	都	忙	课課	进進	坐					

Supplementary Characters

	A	B	C	D	E	F	G	H	I	J
1	拿	出	笔筆	纸紙	打	开開	合	站	起	
2	丁	方	王	陈陳	马馬	谢謝				
3	对對	安	要	了						

#	Character	Radical	Stroke Order							Example
1	这 / 這 zhè	辶 to run	、一亡文文这这							这是…
			、一二三言言言言這							這是…
2	位 wèi	亻 people	丿亻亻位位位位							这位 / 這位
3	是 shì	日 sun	丨口日日旦早早昰是							这位是… / 這位是…
4	老 lǎo	耂 old	一十土耂耂老							丁老师 / 丁老師
5	师 / 師 shī	巾 napkin	丿丨丨丨师师							这位是丁老师
			丿亻亻亻自自師師師							這位是丁老師

6	你 nǐ	亻 people	ノ亻亻伫伫你你						你们 你們

7	们 們 men	亻 people	ノ亻亻们们 / ノ亻亻伊伊伊伊們們						我们 我們

8	好 hǎo	女 female	く女女女好好						你好

9	您 nín	心 heart	ノ亻亻伫伫你你你您您您						您贵姓？ 您貴姓？

10	我 wǒ	戈 spear	ノ二千手我我我						我们 我們

11	来 來 lái	人 people	一 厂 厂 厂 叮 叮 平 来 来							来,…… 來,……
12	介 jiè	人 people	ノ 人 介 介							中介
13	绍 紹 shào	纟/糸 silk	ㄑ ㄑ ㄠ ㄠ 纟 纟 绍 绍 绍 ㄑ ㄑ ㄠ ㄠ 纟 糸 紀 紹 紹 紹							介绍 介紹
14	下 xià	一 one	一 丁 下							一下儿 一下兒
15	儿 兒 ér	儿 child	ノ 儿 ノ 亻 亻 闩 臼 臼 兒							一下儿 一下兒

45

16	姓 xìng	女 female	く夕女女奷奷姓姓	
			姓 姓 姓 姓 姓 姓 姓	你姓……
			姓 姓 姓 姓 姓 姓 姓	
17	叫 jiào	口 mouth	丨口口叫叫	
			叫 叫 叫 叫 叫 叫 叫	他叫小来 他叫小來
			叫 叫 叫 叫 叫 叫 叫	
18	小 xiǎo	小 small	丨小小	
			小 小 小 小 小 小 小	小人
			小 小 小 小 小 小 小	
19	朋 péng	月 moon	丿月月月朋朋朋朋	
			朋 朋 朋 朋 朋 朋 朋	朋友
			朋 朋 朋 朋 朋 朋 朋	
20	友 yǒu	又 again	一ナ方友	
			友 友 友 友 友 友 友	朋友
			友 友 友 友 友 友 友	

#	Character	Radical	Stroke Order	Example
21	什 甚 shén	亻 people	ノ亻仁什 一十廿甘甘其其其甚	什么 甚麼
22	么 麽 me	麻 hemp	ノ厶么 、一广广广庐庐府府麻麻麽麽	你叫什么 你叫甚麼
23	他 tā	亻 people	ノ亻仁他他	他们 他們
24	她 tā	女 female	乚ㄑ女如如她	她们 她們
25	请 請 qǐng	讠/言 word	、讠讠讠讠讠请请请请 、一一言言言言言訁訁訁請請請請	请来一下儿 請來一下兒

26	问 問 wèn	口 mouth	`丶 冂 门 问 问 问` `丨 冂 冂 冂 冃 閂 閂 門 門 問 問`							请问 請問

27	先 xiān	儿 child	`丿 亠 卅 生 失 先`							先生

28	生 shēng	生 produce	`丿 亠 竺 生 生`							先生

29	名 míng	口 mouth	`丿 ク 夕 夕 名 名`							姓名

30	字 zì	宀 roof	`丶 丶 宀 宁 字 字`							名字

#	Character	Radical	Stroke order	Examples
31	姐 jiě	女 female	ㄑ ㄠ 女 刘 如 妈 姐 姐	小姐,姐姐
32	贵 貴 guì	贝/貝 shell	丶 口 口 中 虫 串 昔 贵 贵 丶 口 口 中 虫 串 昔 青 昔 貴 貴	您贵姓,很贵 您貴姓,很貴
33	吗 嗎 ma	口 mouth	丨 口 口 吖 吗 吗 丨 口 口 口⁻ 口⁼ 吁 嗎 嗎 嗎 嗎 嗎	你好吗? 你好嗎?
34	的 de	白 white	ノ イ 白 白 白 的 的	我的
35	女 nǚ	女 female	ㄑ ㄠ 女	女朋友

#	Character	Radical	Stroke Order	Examples
36	男 nán	田 field	丶口日日田男男	男朋友
37	汉漢 hàn	水 water	丶丶氵汉汉 / 丶丶氵氵汁汁汁汁汁淉漢漢	汉语 漢語
38	语語 yǔ	讠/言 word	丶讠讠订评评语语语 / 丶一一三言言言訂評語語語語	语言 語言
39	谁誰 shéi	讠/言 word	丶讠讠讠讠讠讠谁谁谁 / 丶一一三言言言言言計計計誰誰	她是谁？ 她是誰？
40	不 bù	一 one	一丆才不	不认识 不認識

41	认認 rèn	讠/言 word	` 讠 讱 认 ` 亠 亍 亖 言 言 訂 訒 訒 認 認 認 認	认人 認人
42	识識 shí	讠/言 word	` 讠 讱 识 识 识 识 ` 亠 亍 亖 言 言 言 訁 訁 訁 訒 諮 諮 諮 識 識 識	认识 認識
43	早 zǎo	日 sun	丨 冂 日 日 旦 早	你早, 早上
44	晚 wǎn	日 sun	丨 冂 日 日 日' 旷 旷 晚 晚 晚 晚	晚上好！
45	上 shàng	一 one	丨 卜 上	上来 上来

57

46	再 zài	冂 borders	一 厂 厂 冋 冉 再 再							再来 再來

47	见 見 jiàn	目 eye	丨 冂 贝 见 丨 冂 门 月 目 貝 見							再见 再見

48	呢 ne	口 mouth	丨 冂 口 口 叩 叨 呢 呢							我很好，你呢？

49	也 yě	乙 second	丁 九 也							也很好

50	很 hěn	彳 left step	丿 夕 彳 彳 彳 彳 很 很							很好

#	Character	Radical	Stroke Order	Example
51	都 dōu	阝 city	一 十 土 耂 耂 者 者 者 都 都	都很好
52	忙 máng	忄/心 heart	丶 丶 忄 忙 忙 忙	你忙吗? 你忙嗎?
53	课 課 kè	讠/言 word	丶 讠 讠 讠 讠 讠 课 课 课 丶 一 一 亠 亠 言 言 訁 訁 訁 課 課 課	上课 上課
54	进 進 jìn	辶 run	一 二 丰 井 井 讲 进 丿 亻 亻 亻 亻 亻 佳 佳 隹 進 進	请进 請進
55	坐 zuò	土 earth	丿 人 人 从 从 坐 坐	请坐 請坐

NCC Step 1　Pronunciation Exercises

I. Tone discrimination: Circle the right tones you hear.

	A	B
1	wèi	wěi
2	ní	nǐ
3	wǒ	wò
4	xíng	xìng
5	pèng	péng
6	lái	lài
7	guì	guǐ
8	xiàn	xiān
9	qīng wěn	qǐng wèn
10	bù	bú
11	dǐng	dīng
12	qì	qí
13	máng	mǎng
14	shù	shū
15	shǒu	shòu
16	zhān	zhàn
17	hèn	hěn
18	chén	chèn
19	duì	duī
20	dōu	dòu

II. Sound discrimination: Circle the *pinyin* you hear.

	A	B
1	zhè	jì
2	wǎ	wǒ
3	nǐ	lǐ
4	xì	shì
5	hǎo	hǒu
6	lín	nín
7	lái	léi
8	jièshào	jiàoshòu
9	xìng	xìn
10	xiǎo	shǎo
11	páng	péng
12	shéng	shén
13	wàn	wèn
14	xiān	xuān
15	mínzú	míngzi
16	dé	dì
17	lán	nán
18	hàn	hàng
19	yǒu	yǔ
20	qǐ	chǐ
21	fāng	fān
22	wáng	wán
23	chéng	chén
24	xiè	xuè
25	yě	yǐ

	A	B
26	hǎn	hěn
27	duō	dōu
28	wǎn	wǎng
29	mán	máng
30	shàng	sàng
31	shàngkè	shàngge
32	ēn	ān
33	yǒu	yào
34	zuò	zǒu
35	zàn	zhàn
36	qù	chù
37	shǒu	shǎo
38	zǎo	zǒu
39	chī	qī
40	qǐng	qín

67

NCC Step 1　Listening Comprehension Exercises

I. 1) Write down the following questions in *pinyin* or English.
   2) Answer each question in *pinyin*.

1. A:_____?
   B:_____

2. A:_____? _____?
   B:_____

3. A:_____?
   B:_____

4. A:_____?
   B:_____

5. A:_____?
   B:_____

6. A:_____.
   B:_____

7. A:_____?
   B:_____
   A:_____?
   B:_____

NCC Step 1 Listening Comprehension Test

Instruction: Based upon the following dialogues between a man and a woman, determine whether the statements are "True" or "False". Each dialogue will be read twice.

Dialogue I
1. _F_ Mr. Wang knew Miss Ding.
2. _F_ Miss Chen is Miss Ding's teacher.
3. _T_ Miss Chen is Mr. Wang's girl friend.
4. _T_ Miss Chen doesn't know Miss Ding.

Dialogue II
1. _F_ Neither Prof. Yang nor Peter is busy.
2. _F_ Mǎlì (Mary) is Prof. Yang's student.
3. _T_ Peter is Mary's boyfriend.
4. _F_ Mary knew Prof. Yang before.

good
9-22-05

NCC Step 1 In-Class Exercises

Rearrange the following words and phases to make sentences that are grammatically correct; then translate the sentences into English.

1. 贵生 我 你 叫 王 好
   貴生 我 你 叫 王 好

| 你 | 好 | 我 | 叫 | 王 | 贵 | 生 |

2. 方介 一下儿 介绍 我 这是
   方介 一下兒 介紹 我 這是

| 我 | 介绍 | 一 | 下 | 儿 | 这是 | 方 | 介 |

3. 他 呢 是 你 小来
   他 呢 是 你 小來

| 他 | 是 | 小 | 来 | 你 | 呢 |

4. 老师 丁 我 忙 忙 也
   老師 丁 我 忙 忙 也

| 丁 | 老 | 师 | 忙 | 我 | 也 | 忙 |

73

NCC Step 1   Character Exercises

I. Radical recognition: Find the characters with the same radicals and fill in the blanks:
他，她，这/這，位，课/課，你，好，叫，进/進，请/請，们/們，问/問，
吗/嗎，呢，认/認，识/識，晚，姐，谁/誰，语/語

		A	B	C	D	E	F
1	辶						
2	日						
3	女						
4	口						
5	亻						
6	讠/言						

II. Tone differentiation: For each character, give the *pinyin* equivalent in the shaded column.

1	他		她			
2	是		师/師		识/識	
3	姐		介			

III. Distinguish similar characters: For each character, give the *pinyin* equivalent in the shaded column.

1	他		她		也	
2	吗/嗎		呢			
3	不		下			

NCC Step 1   Translation Exercises

1. A: Is he Fang Jie? B: No, he is not. He is Chen Xiaolai.

2. A: Is that man Teacher Ding? B: No, he is not. He is Teacher Wang.

3. A: Is she a teacher? B: No, she is not a teacher. She is a student.

4. A: What is your surname? B: My surname is Fang.

5. A: Is Peter your friend? B: Yes, he is. He is also my teacher.

6. A: May I ask, are you Mr. Xie? B: Yes, my surname is Xie.

7. A: Do you know Guisheng Wang? B: Yes, I know him. Let me introduce (you) briefly.

8. A: Miss Fang is busy. How about Mr. Fang? B: Mr. Fang is also very busy.

9. A: I am called Xiaolai. How about you? B: My name is Anna.

10. A: How are you? B: I am fine. My boyfriend is fine, too.

NCC Step 1   Writing Exercises

Fill in the blanks with the proper words or characters.

1. A:请____,您____ ____?
   B:我____王,____大贵。

2. A:你男朋友____什么名____?
   B:他____丁小三。

3. A:您____丁老师吗?
   B:____不起,我不认____他。
   A:那是____?
   B:那是王老师。

4. A:小王,来,我____ ____一下儿。这____是丁老师。
   B:____好! 丁老师。

5. A:丁先____,早____好!
   B:王小____,你好! 你忙____?
   A:不____忙,你____?
   B:我____不忙。

NCC Step 1   Writing Exercises

Fill in the blanks with the proper words or characters.

1. A:請____,您____ ____?
   B:我____王,____大貴。

2. A:你男朋友____甚麼名____?
   B:他____丁小三。

3. A:您____丁老師嗎?
   B:____不起,我不認____他。
   A:那是____?
   B:那是王老師。

4. A:小王,來,我____ ____一下兒。這____是丁老師。
   B:____好! 丁老師。

5. A:丁先____,早____好!
   B:王小____,你好! 你忙____?
   A:不____忙,你____?
   B:我____不忙。

NCC Step 1 Chapter Exercises

Group: _____ Name: _____

	Characters	Radicals	Phrases	Pinyin	English	Sentences
1	这		这是			
2	那		那位			
3	老		老师			
4	你		你们			
5	好		您好吗			
6	贵		贵姓			
7	什		叫什么			
8	名		名字			
9	朋		男/女朋友			
10	问		请问			
11	先		先生			
12	的		我的			
13	介		介绍一下儿			
14	汉		汉语			
15	认		谁认识			
16	早		早上/晚上			
17	忙		也都很忙			
18	课		上课			
19	进		请进/坐			

NCC Step 1 Chapter Exercises

	Characters	Radicals	Phrases	Pinyin	English	Sentences
1	這		這是			
2	那		那位			
3	老		老師			
4	你		你們			
5	好		您好嗎			
6	貴		貴姓			
7	甚		叫甚麼			
8	名		名字			
9	朋		男/女朋友			
10	問		請問			
11	先		先生			
12	的		我的			
13	介		介紹一下兒			
14	漢		漢語			
15	認		認認識			
16	早		早上/晚上			
17	忙		也都很忙			
18	課		上課			
19	進		請進/坐			

Group: _____ Name: _____

82

Group:_____ Name:_____

New Century Chinese Book I
Step 2: Time & Dates

Homework Assignment List:
Dictation score: ____+____+____+____=____
Homework score: ____+____+____+____=____

Date	NCC I Workbook	NCC I Textbook	Others

Comments:	Suggestions:

83

NCC Step 2   Summary of the Sentence Patterns

Items	Patterns	Sample Sentences
1	Ways of telling time	现在两点(钟)。 现在两点〇五分。 现在两点一刻。 现在两点半。 现在两点三刻。 现在差一刻三点。
2	Dates	二〇〇一年十一月二日/号,星期四 今天几月？几号？星期几？ 一个星期有七天。 一月 vs. 一个月
3	1. 都 (both, all) 2. 都不 (none) 3. 不都 (not all)	1. 我们都学汉语。我们都是好朋友。 2. 他们都不忙。 3. 汉语课的学生不都是中国人。
4	Alternative questions	你学汉语还是英语？ 今天是星期一还是星期二？
5	How many or how much (*inquiring about numbers and quantity*)	一加一等于几？(less than 10) 十乘八等于多少？(more than 10) 你的电话号码是多少(几号)？ 你住多少(几)号？ 你家有几个人？你的汉语班上有多少学生？
6	Which (哪)	你是哪年生的？ 你的生日是哪天？ 你是哪国人？

85

NCC Step 2　Summary of the Sentence Patterns

Items	Patterns	Sample Sentences
1	Ways of telling time	現在兩點(鐘)。 現在兩點〇五分。 現在兩點一刻。 現在兩點半。 現在兩點三刻。 現在差一刻三點。
2	Dates	二〇〇一年十一月二日/號,星期四 今天幾月？幾號？星期幾？ 一個星期有七天。 一月 vs. 一個月
3	1. 都（both, all） 2. 都不（none） 3. 不都（not all）	1. 我們都學漢語。我們都是好朋友。 2. 他們都不忙。 3. 漢語課的學生不都是中國人。
4	Alternative questions	你學漢語還是英語？ 今天是星期一還是星期二？
5	How many or how much (*inquiring about numbers and quantity*)	一加一等於幾？（less than 10） 十乘八等於多少？（more than 10） 你的電話號碼是多少（幾號）？ 你住多少（幾）號？ 你家有幾個人？你的漢語班上有多少學生？
6	Which（哪）	你是哪年生的？ 你的生日是哪天？ 你是哪國人？

NCC Step 2   Characters

Required Characters

	A	B	C	D	E	F	G	H	I	J
1	一	二	三	四	五	六	七	八	九	十
2	百	两兩	第	几幾	多	少	现現	在	点點	分
3	钟鐘	刻	差	午	起	床	还還	中	吃	饭飯
4	睡	觉覺	谢謝	月	星	期	日	天	号號	今
5	明	昨	后後	前	年	去	哪	个個	有	怎
6	样樣	非	常	热熱	冷					

Supplementary Characters

	A	B	C	D	E	F	G	H	I	J
1	北	京	海	广廣	州	桂	林	西		
2	洛	杉	矶磯	旧舊	金	山				
3	夜	表	气氣	时時	间間	到	飞飛	机機		

#	Character	Radical	Stroke Order							Example
1	一 yī	一 one	一							一位
			一	一	一	一	一	一	一	
			一	一	一	一	一	一	一	
2	二 èr	二 two	一二							二十
			二	二	二	二	二	二	二	
			二	二	二	二	二	二		
3	三 sān	一 one	一二三							十三
			三	三	三	三	三	三	三	
			三	三	三	三	三	三		
4	四 sì	口 enclosure	丨冂𠃌四四							四十四
			四	四	四	四	四	四	四	
			四	四	四	四	四	四		
5	五 wǔ	二 two	一丆五五							五十五
			五	五	五	五	五	五	五	
			五	五	五	五	五	五	五	

89

6	六 liù	八 eight	、一六六
7	七 qī	一 one	一七
8	八 bā	八 eight	ノ八
9	九 jiǔ	乙 second	ノ九
10	十 shí	十 ten	一十

六位

七位

八位

九九八十一

十名

#	Character	Radical	Stroke Order							Example
11	百 bǎi	白 white	一 ァ ィ 丙 百 百							一百
12	两 兩 liǎng	入 enter	一 ァ ィ 丙 丙 两 两 一 ァ ィ 币 雨 雨 兩 兩							两百 兩百
13	第 dì	竹 bamboo	ノ ⺀ ⺮ ⺮ ⺮ 竺 笁 笁 第 第							第一名
14	几 幾 jǐ	幺 little	ノ 几 ⺌ ⺌ 幺 ⺹ 幺 幺 丝 线 幾 幾 幾							几百？ 幾百？
15	多 duō	夕 evening	ノ ク 夕 夕 多 多							不多

16	少 shǎo	小 small	丨 丨 小 少						
			少	少	少	少	少	少	多少？
			少	少	少	少	少	少	
17	现 現 xiàn	王 jade	一 二 千 王 玑 玑 现 现						
			一 二 王 玑 玑 玥 珇 玥 現						
			现	现	现	现	现	现	现在 現在
			現	現	現	現	現	現	
18	在 zài	土 earth	一 ナ オ 才 在 在						
			在	在	在	在	在	在	在哪儿？ 在哪兒？
			在	在	在	在	在	在	
19	点 點 diǎn	黑 black	丨 卜 卜 占 占 点 点 点						
			丨 口 曰 曰 甲 里 黑 黑 黑 黠 點 點 點						
			点	点	点	点	点	点	两点 兩點
			點	點	點	點	點	點	
20	分 fēn	刀 knife	丿 八 分 分						
			分	分	分	分	分	分	十分
			分	分	分	分	分	分	

#	Character	Radical	Stroke order	Example
21	钟 鐘 zhōng	钅/金 metal	ノ ㄑ ㄠ ㄠ 乍 钅 钅' 钟' 钟 ノ ㄑ ㄠ ㄠ 乍 乍 乍 金 金 金' 钅' 钅' 铲 铲 镄 镄 鐘 鐘 鐘	几点钟？ 幾點鐘？
22	刻 kè	刀 knife	、 一 亠 亥 亥 亥 刻 刻	七点三刻 七點三刻
23	差 chà	工 work	、 丷 丷 ⺷ 兰 羊 羊 差 差	差一刻七点 差一刻七點
24	午 wǔ	十 ten	ノ 亠 二 午	上午
25	起 qǐ	走 walk	一 十 土 キ キ 赤 走 起 起 起	起来 起來

#	Character	Radical	Stroke order								Examples
26	床 chuáng	木 wood	丶一广广庄床床								起床
27	还還 hái	辶 run	一ㄣ不不不还还								还是 還是
			丨ㄇㄇ罒罒罒罒罒罗罩睘睘環環還								
28	中 zhōng	丨 vertical stroke	丨ㄇ口中								中午
29	吃 chī	口 mouth	丨ㄇ口ㄖ吃吃								吃饭 吃飯
30	饭飯 fàn	饣/食 food	丿𠂊饣饣饭饭								吃中/午饭 吃中/午飯
			丿𠂊𠂊亽今今食食飠飠飯飯								

99

| 31 | 睡 shuì | 目 eye | 丨 冂 冃 目 目 盯 盯 盯 盯 睡 睡 睡 睡 | 睡覺 |

| 32 | 觉 覺 jiào | 见/見 see | 丶 丨 丬 丬 丬 学 学 觉 觉
 丶 丨 丬 丬 丬 丬 丬 睍 睍 睍 睍 與 學 學 覺 覺 覺 覺 覺 | 睡午觉
 睡午覺 |

| 33 | 谢 謝 xiè | 讠/言 word | 丶 讠 讠 讠 讠 讠 讠 讠 讠 讠 谢 谢
 丶 一 二 亠 言 言 訁 訁 訃 訃 謝 謝 謝 謝 謝 謝 | 谢谢
 謝謝 |

| 34 | 月 yuè | 月 moon | 丿 几 月 月 | 一月 |

| 35 | 星 xīng | 日 sun | 丨 冂 日 日 旦 星 星 星 星 | 五星 |

36	期 qī	月 moon	一十卄廿甘其其其期期期期	
			期 期 期 期 期 期 期	星期一
			期 期 期 期 期 期 期	
37	日 rì	日 sun	丨冂日日	
			日 日 日 日 日 日 日	星期日/天
			日 日 日 日 日 日	
38	天 tiān	大 big	一二千天	
			天 天 天 天 天 天 天	一天，天天
			天 天 天 天 天 天 天	
39	号 號 hào	虍 tiger	丨口口叧号 丨口口叧号号'号号'号号號號號	
			号 号 号 号 号 号 号	一月一号 一月一號
			号 号 号 号 号 号 号	
40	今 jīn	人 people	一二キ井'井讲进	
			今 今 今 今 今 今 今	今天
			今 今 今 今 今 今 今	

103

41	明 míng	日 sun	丨 冂 日 日 日' 明 明 明	明天
42	昨 zuó	日 sun	丨 冂 日 日 日' 昨 昨 昨 昨	昨天
43	后 後 hòu	彳 left step	一 厂 广 斤 后 后 丿 夕 彳 彳 行 行 徉 後 後	后天 後天
44	前 qián	刂 knife	丶 丷 䒑 广 广 广 前 前 前	前天
45	年 nián		丿 广 仁 仁 丘 年	今年

46	去 qù	厶 private	一十土去去	去年
47	哪 nǎ	口 mouth	丨口口叮叨叨叨哪哪	哪年?
48	个個 gè	人/亻 people	丿人个 丿亻亻们们們們個個個	几个? 幾個?
49	有 yǒu	月 moon	一ナ才有有有	一年有多少天?
50	怎 zěn	心 heart	丿丆卢乍乍怎怎怎怎	怎么去? 怎麼去?

51	样 様 yàng	木 wood	一十十木木术栏栏栏样 一十十木木术栏栏栏栏样様様様	怎么样? 怎麼樣?
52	非 fēi	非 not	ノ丿ヲヲ⻄非非非	非人
53	常 cháng	巾 napkin	丶丷丬⺌ⵯ尚常常常常常	非常
54	热 熱 rè	灬 fire	一十才扌执执执热热热 一十土去夫去幸幸刲执熱熱熱熱	很热 很熱
55	冷 lěng	冫 ice	丶冫冫冫冷冷冷	今天冷吗? 今天冷嗎?

109

NCC Step 2   Pronunciation Exercises

I. Tone discrimination: Circle the right tones you hear.

	A	B
1	líng	lìng
2	èr	ér
3	yī	yī
4	liù	liú
5	liǎng	lián
6	děng	dèng
7	xiàn	xiǎn
8	diān	diàn
9	kè	kě
10	chá	chà
11	fàn	fǎn
12	xié	xiè
13	běi	bēi
14	qián	qiǎn
15	yǒu	yóu
16	fēicháng	féi cháng
17	nǐ hǎo	ní háo
18	nǐ ne	nì nè
19	qíngtiān	qīngtiān
20	jiēshao	jièshào

II. Sound discrimination: Circle the *pinyin* you hear.

	A	B
1	qī	jī
2	chéng	zhéng
3	qiǎn	jiǎn
4	diǎn	tiǎn
5	cháng	chuáng
6	chī	zhī
7	guǎng	kuáng
8	guī	kuī
9	jiā	chā
10	fēizi	fēijī
11	qián	xián
12	xiāng	shāng
13	yè	rè
14	jīn	qīn
15	sān	shān
16	chà	zà
17	nián	niáng
18	xiàwǔ	xiàhu
19	wǎngshang	wǎnshang
20	rì	rè
21	liǎng	lián
22	děngyú	děngyóu

NCC Step 2 Listening Comprehension Exercises

I. Write down the following mathematic questions in English and give the answers.

1. _____ 2. _____

3. _____ 4. _____

5. _____ 6. _____

II. Translate the following dialogues into English.

1. A: _____

   B: _____

2. A: _____

   B: _____

3. A: _____

   B: _____

III. 1) Write down the following questions in English.
   2) Based on the brief daily schedule on p. 35 or p. 48-49 (character version), answer the questions in *pinyin*.

1. Q: _____

   A: _____

2. Q: _____

   A: _____

3. Q: _____

   A: _____

IV. 1) Write down the following questions in *pinyin* or English.
   2) Based on the flight schedule on p. 36 or p. 50-51 (character version), answer the questions in *pinyin*.

1. Q: _____

   A: _____

115

2. Q:_____

   A:_____

3. Q:_____

   A:_____

Ⅴ. 1) Write down the following dialogues in *pinyin*.
   2) Translate them into English.

   A:_____

   _____

   B:_____

   _____

   A:_____

   _____

   B:_____

   _____

NCC Step 2 Listening Comprehension Test

Instruction: Based upon the following dialogues between a man and a woman, determine whether the statements are "True" or "False". Each dialogue will be read twice.

Dialogue I 1. ____ The man's birthday was last week.
2. ____ The man's birthday is on July 12.
3. ____ This year the man's birthday was on Friday.
4. ____ The woman was born in 1968.

Dialogue II 1. ____ The weather in Beijing in October is neither cold nor hot.
2. ____ The weather in Beijing is a little bit cold in November.
3. ____ The weather in LA is neither cold nor hot in November.

Dialogue III 1. ____ The airplane is taking off at 2:30 a. m.
2. ____ The time now is 1:45 p. m.
3. ____ The Flight 123 is from L. A. to Beijing.

NCC Step 2　Character Exercises

I. Radical recognition: Find the characters with the same radicals and fill in the blanks.

分, 样/樣, 明, 吃, 谢/謝, 早, 星, 汉/漢, 昨, 前, 刻, 怎, 热/熱, 您

		A	B	C	D
1	灬				
2	刀				
3	日				
4	口				
5	讠/言				
6	心				
7	木				
8	氵				

II. Distinguish homonyms: Give the correct character to complete each phrase.

1	zài	现/現____	____见/見
2	yǒu	朋____	____点儿/點兒
3	zhōng	分____	____午
4	qī	星____	____十
5	míng	姓____	____天
6	kè	上____	三____

III. Distinguish similar characters: For each character, give the *pinyin* equivalent in the shaded column.

1	这/這		少		朋	
2	还/還		小		明	

121

NCC Step 2   Translation Exercises

1. A: Is his surname Wang or Ding?   B: His surname is Ding.

2. A: Will you come today or tomorrow?   B: I will come tomorrow.

3. A: Is this month October or November?   B: This month is October.

4. A: Is now seven o'clock or eight o'clock?   B: It's eight o'clock.

5. A: Will you ask Prof. Wang or Prof. Ding?   B: I'll ask Prof. Wang.

6. A: Is your class over at two or three?   B: It's over at ten to two.

7. A: Is next Friday October 25th or 26th?   B: Next Friday is Oct. 26th.

8. A: Are you having dinner at 7:00 or 8:00?   B: Neither. I will have dinner at 7:30.

9. A: When does the Flight 457 take off?   B: 12:45 p.m.

10. A: Do you have class in the morning or afternoon?

    B: I have class in the morning, not in the afternoon.

123

NCC Step 2　Writing Exercises

Fill in the blanks with the proper words or characters.

1. A：小王，三_____六等于_____？
   B：等于九。
   A：三_____九等于_____ _____？
   B：等于二十七。

2. A：小王，你的表现在_____ _____？
   B：三_____一刻。

3. A：你七点_____床还是七点十分_____床？
   B：七点_____。

4. A：北京到上海的飞机几点起_____？
   B：_____一刻两点。

5. A：今天_____月，_____号，星_____ _____？
   B：今天_____。

6. A：北京十月的_____ _____怎么样？
   B：非常好，不_____也不_____。

125

NCC Step 2   Writing Exercises

Fill in the blanks with the proper words or characters.

1. A:小王,三_____六等於_____?
   B:等於九。
   A:三_____九等於_____ _____?
   B:等於二十七。

2. A:小王,你的錶現在_____ _____?
   B:三_____一刻。

3. A:你七點_____床還是七點十分_____床?
   B:七點_____。

4. A:北京到上海的飛機幾點起_____?
   B:_____一刻兩點。

5. A:今天_____月,_____號,星_____ _____?
   B:今天_____。

6. A:北京十月的_____ _____怎麼樣?
   B:非常好,不_____也不_____。

126

NCC Step 2　Special Topic Exercises

Notes

一月(January)　　vs.　　一个月(one month)
去(past)　　　　 vs.　　昨(used in "yesterday")
前(before)　　　 vs.　　后(after/later)
上(up)　　　　　vs.　　下(down)

Answer the following questions in characters:

	Questions	Answers
1	一年有多少天？	
2	一年有多少个月？	
3	十月有多少天？	
4	十月有几个星期日/天？	
5	一个星期有几天？	
6	今年是哪一年？去年呢？	

NCC Step 2   Special Topic Exercises

Notes

一月(January)	vs.	一個月(one month)
去(past)	vs.	昨(used in "yesterday")
前(before)	vs.	後(after/later)
上(up)	vs.	下(down)

Answer the following questions in <u>characters</u>:

	Questions	Answers
1	一年有多少天？	
2	一年有多少個月？	
3	十月有多少天？	
4	十月有幾個星期日/天？	
5	一個星期有幾天？	
6	今年是哪一年？去年呢？	

NCC Step 2 Chapter Exercises

Group: _____ Name: _____

	Characters	Radicals	Phrases	Pinyin	English	Sentences
1	现		现在			
2	点		几点(钟)			
3	分		十分(钟)			
4	刻		三刻(钟)			
5	半		一点半			
6	差		差一刻两点			
7	午		上/中/下午			
8	起		起床			
9	还		还是			
10	吃		吃晚饭			
11	睡		睡觉			
12	星		星期日			
13	号		几号/日			
14	今		今天			
15	明		明年			
16	后		后/前年			
17	个		下个月			
18	怎		怎么样			
19	常		非常热/冷			
20	有		有点儿			

NCC Step 2 Chapter Exercises

Group: _____ Name: _____

	Characters	Radicals	Phrases	*Pinyin*	English	Sentences
1	現		現在			
2	點		幾點(鐘)			
3	分		十分(鐘)			
4	刻		三刻(鐘)			
5	半		一點半			
6	差		差一刻兩點			
7	午		上/中/下午			
8	起		起床			
9	還		還是			
10	吃		吃晚飯			
11	睡		睡覺			
12	星		星期日			
13	號		幾號/日			
14	今		今天			
15	明		明年			
16	後		後/前年			
17	個		下個月			
18	怎		怎麼樣			
19	常		非常熱/冷			
20	有		有點兒			

130

Group:_____ Name:_____

New Century Chinese Book I
Step 3: About Your Classmates

Homework Assignment List:
Dictation score: _____ + _____ + _____ + _____ = _____
Homework score: _____ + _____ + _____ + _____ = _____

Date	NCC I Workbook	NCC I Textbook	Others

Comments: **Suggestions:**

NCC Step 3 Summary of the Sentence Patterns

Items	Patterns	Sample Sentences
1	哪儿 Where	你住在哪儿？ 你在哪儿住？ 你是在哪儿生的？
2	是…的。(*focusing on the location*) (*focusing on the time*) (*focusing on the purpose*) (*focusing on the subject*)	她是在美国出生的。 她是去年去中国的。 她去中国是学汉语的。 是她去年在北京大学学汉语的。
3	How many or how much (*inquiring about people's age*)	小朋友，你今年几岁？ 王先生，请问您今年多大？ 老先生，请问您今年多大岁数？
4	Affirmative/Negative questions (the "V.＋不＋V." structure)	你忙不忙？ 他是不是老师？ 你说不说汉语？ 你有没有妹妹？
5	可是 But, however	我说汉语，可是不认识汉字。 他爸爸是美国人，可是他妈妈是中国人。

NCC Step 3　Summary of the Sentence Patterns

Items	Patterns	Sample Sentences
1	哪兒 Where	你住在哪兒？ 你在哪兒住？ 你是在哪兒生的？
2	是…的。(*focusing on the location*) 　　　　(*focusing on the time*) 　　　　(*focusing on the purpose*) 　　　　(*focusing on the subject*)	她是在美國出生的。 她是去年去中國的。 她去中國是學漢語的。 是她去年在北京大學學漢語的。
3	How many or how much (*inquiring about people's age*)	小朋友，你今年幾歲？ 王先生，請問您今年多大？ 老先生，請問您今年多大歲數？
4	Affirmative/Negative questions (the "V.＋不＋V." structure)	你忙不忙？ 他是不是老師？ 你說不說漢語？ 你有沒有妹妹？
5	可是 But, however	我說漢語，可是不認識漢字。 他爸爸是美國人，可是他媽媽是中國人。

NCC Step 3 Characters

Required Characters

	A	B	C	D	E	F	G	H	I	J
1	言	人	那	同	国國	家	说說	学學	习習	可
2	文	岁歲	数數	太	爸	妈媽	住	宿	舍	电電
3	话話	码碼	出	地	留	身	证證	性	别	址
4	德	俄	法	美	本	英				
5										
6										

Supplementary Characters

	A	B	C	D	E	F	G	H	I	J
1	民	族								
2	层層	楼樓								
3	身	高	体體	重	公	班	候	失	踪蹤	员員

#	Character	Radical	Stroke Order	Examples
1	言 yán	言 word	、一 亠 宁 言 言 言	语言 / 語言
2	人 rén	人 people	ノ 人	大人
3	那 nà	阝 city	フ ヨ ヨ 月 那 那	那个 / 那個
4	同 tóng	冂 borders	丨 冂 冂 同 同 同	同学 / 同學
5	国 / 國 guó	囗 enclosure	丨 冂 冂 冃 用 囯 国 国 丨 冂 冂 冋 冋 同 同 或 國 國 國	中国 / 中國

#	Character	Radical	Stroke order	Examples
6	家 jiā	宀 roof	丶丶宀宀宀宁穸家家家	大家, 国家 大家, 國家
7	说說 shuō	言 word	丶讠讠讠讠讠说说说 丶二亠言言言言訁訁訁說說	你说什么? 你說甚麼?
8	学學 xué	子 child	丶丷丷丷丷学学学 丨丨ff ff fF fF 闩 鬥 鬥 與 學 學 學	学什么? 學甚麼?
9	习習 xí	羽 feather	丁 刁 习 丁 刁 习 刁 羽 羽 羽 習 習 習	学习汉语 學習漢語
10	可 kě	口 mouth	一 丆 冂 可 可	可是

139

11	文 wén	文 literature	丶一ナ文	文 文 文 文 文 文 文 文 文 文 文 文 文 文	中文
12	岁 歲 suì	止 stop	丨止山屮岁岁 丨⺊止此此些芦芦芦芦荿歲歲	岁 岁 岁 岁 岁 岁 岁 歲 歲 歲 歲 歲 歲 歲	你几岁？ 你幾歲？
13	数 數 shù	攵 tap	丶丷丷⺷米米籵籵斢斢数数 丶口曰旦串串串婁婁婁數數數	数 数 数 数 数 数 数 數 數 數 數 數 數 數	岁数 歲數
14	太 tài	大 big	一ナ大太	太 太 太 太 太 太 太 太 太 太 太 太 太 太	太多
15	爸 bà	父 father	ノハグ父交爷爸爸	爸 爸 爸 爸 爸 爸 爸 爸 爸 爸 爸 爸 爸 爸	爸爸

141

#	Character	Radical	Stroke Order	Example
16	妈 妈 mā	女 female	乚 𠃌 女 妇 妈妈 乚 𠃌 女 妇 妒 妒 妒 媽媽媽媽媽	妈妈 媽媽
17	住 zhù	亻 people	丿 亻 亻 丿 住 住 住	住多少号？ 住多少號？
18	宿 sù	宀 roof	丶 丷 宀 宀 宀 宀 宿 宿 宿	宿舍
19	舍 shè	舌 tongue	丿 人 𠆢 𠆢 𠆢 𠆢 舍 舍	学生宿舍 學生宿舍
20	电 電 diàn	雨 rain	丨 冂 日 电 一 冖 宀 雨 雨 雨 雨 雨 雷 電	电话 電話

21	话話 huà	言 word	丶 亠 讠 订 计 汢 话话话						说话 説話
			丶 亠 亠 言 言 言 訁 訂 許 評 話話						
22	码碼 mǎ	石 rock	一 ア 厂 石 石 石 码 码						号码 號碼
			一 ア 厂 石 石 石 石 石 砰 碼 碼 碼 碼						
23	出 chū	凵 receptacle	一 凵 屮 出 出						出生
24	地 dì	土 earth	一 十 土 圠 地 地						出生地
25	留 liú	田 field	丶 ㄏ 乊 印 切 卯 甾 留 留						留学生 留學生

145

26	身 shēn	身 body	´ ⺁ ⺁ 斤 自 自 身 身		一身
27	证 證 zhèng	讠/言 word	` 讠 讠 讠 讠 证 证 证 ` 亠 ㇊ 言 言 言 言 訁 訁 訊 訊 誣 誣 證 證 證 證		身份证 身份證
28	性 xìng	忄 heart	` ` 忄 忄 忄 忄 性 性		人性
29	别 bié	刂 knife	` ⺉ 口 口 号 另 别 别		性别
30	址 zhǐ	土 earth	一 十 土 圵 圵 址 址		地址, 住址

147

#	Character	Radical	Stroke Order	Examples
31	德 dé	彳 left step	ノ ノ 彳 彳 彳 彳 徍 徍 徲 徳 德 德 德	德国, 德文 / 德國, 德文
32	俄 é	亻 people	ノ 亻 亻 亻 仟 佢 俄 俄 俄	俄国, 俄语 / 俄國, 俄語
33	法 fǎ	氵 water	丶 丶 氵 氵 汁 泮 法 法	法国, 法语 / 法國, 法語
34	美 měi	羊 sheep	丶 丶 丷 ⺷ ⺷ 羊 羔 美 美	美国 / 美國
35	本 běn	木 wood	一 十 オ 木 本	日本, 日语 / 日本, 日語

149

| 36 | 英 yīng | 艹 grass | 一 十 艹 艹 艹 荁 荚 英 | | | | | | 英国，英语
英國，英語 |

NCC Step 3 Listening Comprehension Exercises

I. Write down the following dialogues in *pinyin*.

   1. A: _____

      B: _____

   2. A: _____

      B: _____

   3. A: _____

      B: _____

II. Based upon Activity 8 (p. 73 or p. 85):
   1) Write down the questions in *pinyin*.
   2) Answer the questions in <u>characters</u>.

   1. Q: _____

      A: _____

   2. Q: _____

      A: _____

   3. Q: _____

      A: _____

   4. Q: _____

      A: _____

   5. Q: _____

      A: _____

NCC Step 3 Listening Comprehension Test

Instruction: Based upon the following dialogues between a man and a woman, determine whether the statements are "True" or "False". Each dialogue will be read twice.

Dialogue I
1. ____ The man knew the woman's friend before.
2. ____ Tianzhong speaks Japanese and Chinese.
3. ____ The woman is Mr. Tianzhong's teacher.

Dialogue II
1. ____ Both the man and the woman live in dormitory.
2. ____ The woman lives on the 5th floor.
3. ____ The man's home number is (949) 813-8846.

Dialogue III
1. ____ The man was born in L. A.
2. ____ The woman is studying in Beijing.
3. ____ Both Mr. & Mrs. Ding are fluent in French.
4. ____ The woman is fluent in Chinese.

NCC Step 3   Character Exercises

I. Radical recognition: Find the characters with the same radicals and fill in the blanks:

说/說，得，男，法，俄，忙，妈/媽，宿，语/語，地，很，留，份，证/證，性，别，住，址，安，娜，李，家

		A	B	C
1	讠/言	说	语	证
2	氵	法		
3	女	妈	娜	
4	田	男	留	
5	心			
6	亻/人	俄	份	住
7	木	李		
8	刂/刀	别		
9	土	法	地	址
10	宀	宿	家	安
11	彳	得	很	

II. Distinguish similar characters: For each character, give the *pinyin* equivalent in the shaded column.

1	大		太	
2	吗/嗎		妈/媽	
3	地		他	
4	第		弟	
5	说/説		话/話	

157

Ⅲ. Tone differentiation: Give the *pinyin* equivalent to each character.

1	ren	人____	认/認____	
2	wen	问____	文____	
3	xing	姓____	性____	
4	di	第____	地____	
5	de	的____	德____	
6	shen	什____	身____	
7	dian	点/點____	电/電____	
8	fen	分____	份____	
9	ba	八____	爸____	
10	xian	先____	现/現____	
11	liu	六____	留____	
12	ke	课/課____	刻____	可____
13	ma	妈/媽____	吗/嗎____	码/碼____
14	na	那____	哪____	娜____
15	you	友____	有____	又____

159

NCC Step 3   Translation Exercises

1. A: What is your student ID number?   B: My Student ID number is 987-654-321.
   Ni de zhengjian shi duo sao   Wo de zhengjian shi ...

2. A: What is your telephone number?   B: My telephone number is (949)824-2678.
   Ni de hao ma duo sao?   Wo de hao ma shi ...

3. A: How old is your teacher?   B: She is twenty four.
   Ni de lao shi duo da?   Ta shi er shi

4. A: Where is he from?   B: He is from Beijing.
   Ta shi na guo ren?   Ta .

5. A: Is today Friday? (A not A Q)   B: No, today is Thursday, not Friday.
   Zin tran shi bu shi xing qi wu.   Bu shi, zin tian shi xing qi shi, bu shi xing qi wu.

6. A: Did she come to study Chinese? (shi...de)   B: No, she came to study English.

7. A: Are you American?   B: Yes, I am American-born Chinese.
   Ni shi mei guo ren ma?   Wo shi mei guo sheng de zhong guo ren ABC

8. A: Is Xiao Wang your classmate?   B: Yes, he is my classmate and also my friend.
   Xiao wang shi ni de tong xue ma?   Shi, ta shi wo de tong xue, ye shi wo de peng you.

9. A: Do you study German? (A not A Q)   B: No, I study Chinese. I don't study German.
   Ni xue de guo xuexi bu xue   Wo xue Han Yu xuexi

10. A: Do you speak Chinese or not?   B: Yes, I do.
    Ni shuo zhong wen ma   Wo shuo.

NCC Step 3   Writing Exercises

Fill in the blanks with the proper words or characters.

1. A：那是____？
   B：我也不认识。他是不是法____ ____？
   A：不是，他说汉____。

2. A：请问，王老师，您今年____ ____？
   B：我四十____，你____ ____？
   A：我今年九岁。

3. B：你住在____ ____？
   A：学生____ ____，二____三０五____。
   B：你的电话____ ____是____ ____？
   A：是_____。

4. A：你的身____ ____号码是多少？
   B：_____。
   A：你是哪年出____的？
   B：一九____ ____ ____。
   A：你是在哪儿出____的？
   B：在____国洛杉矶。

5. A：请问，你的____高是多少？
   B：五____六____。
   A：你的____ ____呢？
   B：一百二十五____。

163

NCC Step 3　Writing Exercises

Fill in the blanks with the proper words or characters.

1. A：那是____？
   B：我也不認識。他是不是法____ ____？
   A：不是，他說漢____。

2. A：請問，王老師，您今年____ ____？
   B：我四十____，你____ ____？
   A：我今年九歲。

3. B：你住在____ ____？
   A：學生____ ____，二____三〇五____。
   B：你的電話____ ____是____ ____？
   A：是_____。

4. A：你的身____ ____號碼是多少？
   B：_____。
   A：你是哪年出____的？
   B：一九____ ____ ____。
   A：你是在哪兒出____的？
   B：在____國洛杉磯。

5. A：請問，你的____高是多少？
   B：五____六____。
   A：你的____ ____呢？
   B：一百二十五____。

NCC Step 3　Special Topic Exercises 是…的

	问题	用中文回答
1	你今天是几点起床的？	
2	你是哪年(出)生的？	
3	你是几月认识你的汉语老师的？	
4	你是几岁上大学的？	
5	你今天是从哪儿来学院的？	
6	你是怎么来学院的？	
7	你昨天是跟谁一起学习的？	
8	是谁每天教你中文的？	
9	你每天来学院是做什么的？	

小王昨天跟她男朋友一起坐车去LA看了一场电影。
　1　 2　　　 3　　　 4　 5　　　　 6

	用中文问问题
1	
2	小王是哪天去LA的？
3	
4	
5	
6	

NCC Step 3　Special Topic Exercises 是…的

	問題	用中文回答
1	你今天是幾點起床的？	
2	你是哪年(出)生的？	
3	你是幾月認識你的漢語老師的？	
4	你是幾歲上大學的？	
5	你今天是從哪兒來學院的？	
6	你是怎麼來學院的？	
7	你昨天是跟誰一起學習的？	
8	是誰每天教你中文的？	
9	你每天來學院是做甚麼的？	

小王昨天跟她男朋友一起坐車去LA看了一場電影。
　1　　2　　　　3　　　　4　　5　　　　　6

	用中文問問題
1	
2	小王是哪天去LA的？
3	
4	
5	
6	

NCC Step 3 Special Topic Exercises

北京大学留学生证

姓名:王马克
性别:男
住址:北京大学留学生宿舍二层十一号
电话:86-10-859-4237
有效日期:2003 年 6 月 31 日

出生日期:1980 年 2 月 18 日
出生地点:美国洛杉矶
身高:6 呎 2 吋
体重:170 磅
国籍:美国
证号:0697832

I. Please sort out the information from the student I. D. above and fill out the following table:

	English (*Pinying*)	*Pinyin*	English
1	Name ( )		
2	Gender ( )		
3	Age ( )		
4	Birthday ( )		
5	Birth place ( )		
6	Nationality ( )		
7	Address ( )		
8	Phone No. ( )		
9	Height ( )	____ chǐ ____ cùn	
10	Weight ( )	_____ bàng	
11	Expiration date ( )	yǒuxiàorìqī	

NCC Step 3 Special Topic Exercises

北京大學留學生証

姓名：王馬克　　　　　　出生日期：1980 年 2 月 18 日
性別：男　　　　　　　　出生地點：美國洛杉磯
住址：北京大學留學生宿舍二層十一號　　身高：6 呎 2 吋
　　　　　　　　　　　　體重：170 磅
電話：86-10-859-4237　　國籍：美國
有效日期：2003 年 6 月 31 日　　証號：0697832

Ⅰ. Please sort out the information from the student I. D. above and fill out the following table:

	English (*Pinying*)	*Pinyin*	English
1	Name ( )		
2	Gender ( )		
3	Age ( )		
4	Birthday ( )		
5	Birth place ( )		
6	Nationality ( )		
7	Address ( )		
8	Phone No. ( )		
9	Height ( )	___ chǐ ___ cùn	
10	Weight ( )	_____ bàng	
11	Expiration date ( )	yǒuxiàoriqī	

NCC Step 3   Exercises on the Student ID

	中文	*Pinyin*	English	Asking questions
1	身份证			eg. 你的身份证号码是多少?
2	留学生证			
3	姓名			
4	性别			
5	出生日期			
6	出生地点			
7	___市			
8	大学区			
9	二层二〇八号			
10	民族			
11	国籍			
12	住址/地址			
13	身高			
14	体重			
15	公斤/磅			
16	公分/呎,吋			
17	证件号码			
18	有效日期			

NCC Step 3 Exercises on the Student ID

	中文	*Pinyin*	English	Asking questions
1	身份證			eg. 你的身份證號碼是多少？
2	留學生證			
3	姓名			
4	性別			
5	出生日期			
6	出生地點			
7	___市			
8	大學區			
9	二層二〇八號			
10	民族			
11	國籍			
12	住址/地址			
13	身高			
14	體重			
15	公斤/磅			
16	公分/呎,吋			
17	證件號碼			
18	有效日期			

NCC Step 3　Chapter Exercises

Group: _____ Name: _____

	Characters	Radicals	Phrases	*Pinyin*	English	Sentences
1	人		美国人			
2	语		英语			
3	文		中文			
4	学		同学			
5	习		学习			
6	可		可是			
7	岁		几岁			
8	多		多大			
9	数		岁数			
10	住		住(在)			
11	哪		哪儿			
12	宿		宿舍			
13	电		电话			
14	号		号码			
15	出		出生			
16	地		地点			
17	留		留学生			
18	证		身份证			
19	性		性别			
20	址		住址			

NCC Step 3　Chapter Exercises

Group: _____　Name: _____

	Characters	Radicals	Phrases	*Pinyin*	English	Sentences
1	人		美國人			
2	語		英語			
3	文		中文			
4	學		同學			
5	習		學習			
6	可		可是			
7	歲		幾歲			
8	多		多大			
9	數		歲數			
10	住		住(在)			
11	哪		哪兒			
12	宿		宿舍			
13	電		電話			
14	號		號碼			
15	出		出生			
16	地		地點			
17	留		留學生			
18	證		身份證			
19	性		性別			
20	址		住址			

172

Group:_____ Name:_____

New Century Chinese Book I
Step 4: Descriptions

Homework Assignment List:
Dictation score: _____+_____+_____+_____=_____
Homework score: _____+_____+_____+_____=_____

Date	NCC I Workbook	NCC I Textbook	Others

Comments: **Suggestions:**

NCC Step 4   Summary of the Sentence Patterns

Items	Patterns	Sample Sentences
1	Modification of nouns by clauses with "DE" (S V 的 O or S V O 的 O)	我上的汉语课很好。 我认识那个上汉语课的同学。 我认识的那个同学上汉语课。
2	的 (*the marker of attributes*) 的 (*attribute indicating possession*)	她穿一条红色的裙子。vs. 她穿一条红裙子。 这条裙子是她的。 她的裙子是红的。 这是王小姐的红裙子。 这条很漂亮的红裙子是王小姐妹妹的。 谁的裙子很漂亮? 我的和你的都很好看。
3	Verb 着 Verb$_1$ 着 verb$_2$	王大中穿着一件黑大衣。 她戴着帽子睡觉。

NCC Step 4   Summary of the Sentence Patterns

Items	Patterns	Sample Sentences
1	Modification of nouns by clauses with "DE" (S V 的 O or S V O 的 O)	我上的漢語課很好。 我認識那個上漢語課的同學。 我認識的那個同學上漢語課。
2	的 (*the marker of attributes*) 的 (*attribute indicating possession*)	她穿一條紅色的裙子。vs. 她穿一條紅裙子。 這條裙子是她的。 她的裙子是紅的。 這是王小姐的紅裙子。 這條很漂亮的紅裙子是王小姐妹妹的。 誰的裙子很漂亮？ 我的和你的都很好看。
3	Verb 著 Verb$_1$ 著 verb$_2$	王大中穿著一件黑大衣。 她戴著帽子睡覺。

NCC Step 4   Characters

Required Characters

	A	B	C	D	E	F	G	H	I	J
1	白	黑	红紅	黄	蓝藍	绿綠	颜顏	色	衬襯	衫
2	穿	衣	件	裤褲	子	毛	皮	鞋	裙	双雙
3	条條	袜襪	班	眼	眼	鼻	嘴	巴	耳	朵
4	头頭	发髮	脖	手	脚腳	腰	肚	腿	长長	短
5	粗	细	高	疼	最	哥	弟	妹	矮	和
6	没	胖	瘦	又	金	棕				

Supplementary Characters

	A	B	C	D	E	F	G	H	I	J
1	粉	灰	紫	戴	顶頂	副	领領	带	帽	球
2	眼	镜鏡	漂	亮						
3										

#	字	部首	筆順							詞語
1	白 bái	日 sun	ノ イ 白 白 白							白大衣
2	黑 hēi	灬 fire	ノ 口 回 回 甲 甲 里 黒 黑 黑 黑							黑天
3	紅 紅 hóng	糸/纟 silk	ノ 乙 幺 纟 红 红 / ノ 乙 幺 纟 幺 糸 糸 紅 紅							红色 / 紅色
4	黄 huáng	黄 yellow	一 十 廾 共 苎 苎 苎 黄 黄 黄 黄							黄土
5	蓝 藍 lán	艹 grass	一 十 艹 艹 艹 艹 茈 茈 䕅 蓝 蓝 蓝 / 一 十 艹 艹 艹 艹 艹 茈 茈 䕅 䕅 䕅 藍 藍							蓝天 / 藍天

179

6	绿 綠 lù	纟/糹 silk	乚 幺 纟 纟 红 红 纤 纤 绿 绿 绿 乚 幺 纟 纟 红 红 纤 纤 綠 綠 綠	绿大衣 綠大衣
7	颜 顔 yán	页/頁 page	丶 亠 产 立 产 产 序 彦 彦 彦 彦 彦 颜 颜 丶 亠 产 立 产 产 序 彦 彦 彦 彦 彦 顔 顔 顔 顔	颜色 顔色
8	色 sè	色 color	丿 夕 岁 各 各 色	红色 紅色
9	衬 襯 chèn	衤 clothes	丶 亠 才 衤 衤 衬 衬 丶 亠 才 衤 衤 衤 衤 衤 衤 衤 衤 衤 衤 衤 衤 衤 襯	衬衫 襯衫
10	衫 shān	衤 clothes	丶 亠 才 衤 衤 衫 衫 衫	黄衬衫 黄襯衫

181

#	Character	Radical	Stroke Order							Example
11	穿 chuān	穴 cave	丶丶宀宀宀宁穵穿穿							穿大衣
12	衣 yī	衣 clothes	丶一ナオ衣衣							大衣
13	件 jiàn	亻 people	ノ亻亻仁件件							一件____
14	裤 kù	衤 clothes	丶丶才才礻衤衤衤衤裤裤裤 丶丶才才礻衤衤衤衤衤裤裤裤裤							黄裤子 黄裤子
15	子 zǐ	子 child	丶了子							裤子 裤子

16	毛 máo	毛 fur hair	ノ 二 三 毛	
			毛 毛 毛 毛 毛 毛 毛 毛 毛 毛 毛 毛 毛 毛	毛衣
17	皮 pí	皮 skin leather	一 厂 广 皮 皮	
			皮 皮 皮 皮 皮 皮 皮 皮 皮 皮 皮 皮 皮 皮	皮大衣
18	鞋 xié	革 leather	一 十 廿 世 世 苦 苦 苦 革 革 䩄 靯 鞋 鞋	
			鞋 鞋 鞋 鞋 鞋 鞋 鞋 鞋 鞋 鞋 鞋 鞋 鞋 鞋	皮鞋
19	裙 qún	衤 clothes	丶 ㇇ 丆 孑 衤 衤 衤 衤 衤 裙 裙	
			裙 裙 裙 裙 裙 裙 裙 裙 裙 裙 裙 裙 裙 裙	一____裙子
20	双 雙 shuāng	隹 bird	㇇ 又 双 双 ノ 亻 亻 亻 亻 亻 隹 隹 隹 隹 隹 隹 雙 雙	
			双 双 双 双 双 双 双 雙 雙 雙 雙 雙 雙 雙	两双皮鞋 兩雙皮鞋

21	条 條 tiáo	木 wood	ノク久冬条条 ノイ亻彳伫伀佟條條	两条____ 兩條____
22	袜 襪 wà	衤 clothes	、ブオオネネ衤衤衤袜 、ブオオネネ衤衤衤衤襪襪襪襪襪	一____袜子 一____襪子
23	班 bān	王 jade	一 二 千 王 王 玎 玡 班 班	汉语班 漢語班 班上
24	眼 yǎn	目 eye	丨冂冃目目目'目'目'眼眼眼	眼镜 眼鏡
25	睛 jīng	目 eye	丨冂冃目目目睛睛睛睛睛	黑眼睛

187

#	Character	Radical	Stroke order	Example
26	鼻 bí	鼻 nose	′ ′ 竹 白 白 白 自 鳥 鳥 畠 畠 鼻 鼻	大鼻子
27	嘴 zuǐ	口 mouth	＼ 口 口 口¹ 口¹ 吡 吡 叱 哨 哨 嘴 嘴 嘴	大嘴
28	巴 bā		⁷ ㄋ 卫 巴	嘴巴
29	耳 ěr	耳 ear	一 丆 丌 刐 耳 耳	耳朵
30	朵 duǒ	木 wood	ノ 几 几 孕 朵 朵	两朵 兩朵

189

#	Character	Radical	Stroke order	Practice	Example
31	头 頭 tóu	页/頁 eye	丶丷二头头 一丨丆丙百百豆豆豆豆頭頭頭頭頭頭	头头头头头头 頭頭頭頭頭頭頭	大头 大頭
32	发 髮 jiào	髟 hair	一ナ方发发 一丆丆干干亏長長髟髟髟髮髮	发发发发发发发 髮髮髮髮髮髮	头发 頭髮
33	脖 bó	月 flesh	丿刀月月肜肸胪胪脖脖脖	脖脖脖脖脖脖 脖脖脖脖脖脖脖	红脖子 紅脖子
34	手 shǒu	手 hand	一二三手	手手手手手手手 手手手手手手手	大手
35	脚 腳 jiǎo	月 flesh	丿刀月月肜肸胪胪脚脚脚 丿刀月月月肝肛胪胪腳腳	脚脚脚脚脚脚 腳腳腳腳腳腳腳	小脚 小腳

#	Character	Radical	Stroke Order	Example
36	腰 yāo	月 flesh	ノ 几 月 月 月⼀ 月⼁ 肝 胛 胛 腰 腰 腰	粗腰
37	肚 dù	月 flesh	ノ 几 月 月 月⼀ 肚 肚	大肚子
38	腿 tuǐ	月 flesh	ノ 几 月 月 月⼀ 月⼁ 月⼁ 胆 胆 腿 腿 腿	小腿
39	长/長 cháng	长/長 long	ノ ⼀ 长 长 ⼀ ⼁ ⼁ ⼁ 乍 长 長 長	长鼻子 長鼻子
40	短 duǎn	矢 arrow	ノ ⼀ ⼁ 乍 矢 矢⼀ 知 知 短 短 短	短脖子

193

41	粗 cū	米 rice	丶 丷 ㄎ 半 米 米 籵 籵 粗 粗	
			粗 粗 粗 粗 粗 粗 粗	粗脖子
			粗 粗 粗 粗 粗 粗 粗	
42	细 細 xì	纟/糸 silk	乚 ㄥ 纟 纟 纫 纫 细 细	
			乚 ㄥ 纟 纟 糸 糸 紀 紃 細 細	
			细 细 细 细 细 细	细腰 細腰
			細 細 細 細 細 細 細	
43	高 gāo	高 tall	丶 亠 㐄 古 吉 高 高 高 高	
			高 高 高 高 高 高 高	很高
			高 高 高 高 高 高 高	
44	疼 téng	疒 illness	丶 亠 广 扩 疒 疒 疼 疼 疼 疼	
			疼 疼 疼 疼 疼 疼 疼	脚疼 脚疼
			疼 疼 疼 疼 疼 疼 疼	
45	最 zuì	日 say	丶 冂 日 日 旦 早 昌 昌 冣 最 最	
			最 最 最 最 最 最 最	最好
			最 最 最 最 最 最 最	

#	Character	Radical	Stroke Order	Example
46	哥 gē	口 mouth	一 ㄱ ㄱ 可 可 可 哥 哥 哥 哥	哥哥
47	弟 dì	弓 bow	丶 丷 䒑 䒑 弟 弟 弟	弟弟
48	妹 mèi	女 female	㇄ 夂 女 女 妇 妹 妹 妹	妹妹
49	矮 ǎi	矢 arrow	丿 一 ㄣ 手 矢 矢 矢 矢 矮 矮 矮 矮 矮	七个小矮人 七個小矮人
50	和 hé	口 mouth	丿 一 千 矛 禾 禾 和 和	我和你

51	没 méi	氵 water	丶丶氵氵沪没没	没有
52	胖 pàng	月 flesh	丿𠄌月月月胖胖胖	胖子
53	瘦 shòu	疒 illness	丶一广广疒疒疒疒疒疒瘦瘦	瘦小
54	又 yòu	又 again	𠃋又	又高又大
55	金 jīn	金 gold, metal	丿𠆢𠆢今今全全金金	金发 金髮

56	棕 zōng	木 wood	一 十 才 木 术 术 松 松 松 柊 棕 棕						
		棕	棕	棕	棕	棕	棕	棕	棕色
		棕	棕	棕	棕	棕	棕	棕	

NCC Step 4   Listening Comprehension Exercises

I. Based upon Activity 1: 1) Write down the following questions in *pinyin*. 2) Answer the questions in <u>characters</u> according to the chart in Activity 1 (p. 91 or p. 102).

1. Q: _____

   A: _____

2. Q: _____

   A: _____

3. Q: _____

   A: _____

4. Q: _____

   A: _____

II. Based upon Activity 6: 1) Write down the questions in *pinyin*. 2) Answer the questions in <u>characters</u> according to the picture in Activity 6 (p. 96 or 109).

1. Q: _____

   A: _____

2. Q: _____

   A: _____

3. Q: _____

   A: _____

4. Q: _____

   A: _____

NCC Step 4 Listening Comprehension Test

Instruction: Based upon the following dialogues between a man and a woman, determine whether the statements are "True" or "False". Each dialogue will be read twice.

Dialogue I
1. ____ The white shirt is not long enough.
2. ____ The red shirt is too expensive.
3. ____ The red shirt is perfect in length.

Dialogue II
1. ____ Xiao Wang has no girlfriend now.
2. ____ The girl in red skirt has big eyes and a small mouth.
3. ____ The girl in red skirt is a good student.

Dialogue III
1. ____ The girl is talking to her brother.
2. ____ The girl had stomachache.
3. ____ During this conversation, 5 body parts were mentioned.

Dialogue IV
1. ____ Xiao Wang is the tallest in his class.
2. ____ Xiao Wang is thirteen years old.
3. ____ Xiao Wang has big feet and very long legs.

NCC Step 4　Character Exercises

I. Radical Recognition: Find the characters with the same radicals and fill in the blanks:

肚,裙,胖,瘦,妹,红/紅,脚/腳,蓝/藍,绿/綠,衬/襯,衫,件,矮,条/條,腿,袜/襪,眼,脖,短,睛,细/細,英,棕,腰,嘴,疼,睡,吃

		A	B	C	D	E	F
1	月						
2	衣						
3	女						
4	疒						
5	纟/糹						
6	人						
7	木						
8	口						
9	目						
10	矢						
11	艹						

II. Tone differentiation: Give the *pinyin* equivalent to each character.

1	bai	百 _____	白 _____	
2	yan	言 _____	眼 _____	颜/顏 _____
3	chen	陈/陳 _____	衬/襯 _____	
4	zi	字 _____	子 _____	
5	xie	谢/謝 _____	鞋 _____	
6	er	二 _____	儿 _____	耳 _____
7	duo	多 _____	朵 _____	
8	xi	习/習 _____	细/細 _____	
9	zui	最 _____	嘴 _____	
10	shou	手 _____	瘦 _____	
11	ba	八 _____	巴 _____	爸 _____
12	mei	没 _____	美 _____	妹 _____
13	jiao	叫 _____	脚/腳 _____	教 _____
14	jin	今 _____	进/進 _____	金 _____
15	shan	衫 _____	扇 _____	
16	yi	_____ 条/條	_____ 件	_____ , 二

Ⅲ. Character differentiation: Give the equivalent character to each phrase.

	Shared Sound	Fill in Blanks with Different Characters		
1	yī	大___	___,二,三	
2	jiàn	两___上衣	再___	
3	jīn	___色	___天	公___
4	dì	___弟	___址	___六课

Ⅳ. Fill in the blanks with the appropriate measure words (letters only):

a. 件　b. 条　c. 双　d. 只　e. 副　f. 顶

1	两___衬衫	7	两___裙子
2	两___裤子	8	两___鞋子
3	两___袜子	9	两___毛衣
4	两___帽子	10	两___大衣
5	两___领带	11	两___皮鞋
6	两___眼镜	12	两___上衣

Ⅲ. Character differentiation：Give the equivalent character to each phrase.

	Shared Sound	Fill in Blanks with Different Characters		
1	yī	大____	____,二,三	
2	jiàn	兩____上衣	再____	
3	jīn	____色	____天	公____
4	dì	____弟	____址	____六課

Ⅳ. Fill in the blanks with the appropriate measure words (letters only)：

a. 件　b. 條　c. 雙　d. 隻　e. 副　f. 頂

1	兩____襯衫	7	兩____裙子
2	兩____褲子	8	兩____鞋子
3	兩____襪子	9	兩____毛衣
4	兩____帽子	10	兩____大衣
5	兩____領帶	11	兩____皮鞋
6	兩____眼鏡	12	兩____上衣

NCC Step 4   Translation Exercises

1. A: Whose shoes are these? B: This pair of shoes is mine.

2. A: How many white skirts do you have? B: I have two.

3. A: Is she a good Chinese teacher? B: Yes, she is a good Chinese teacher.

4. A: Who is the man wearing a sweater? B: That's Xiao Wang.

5. A: Which shirt is your friend's? B: That yellow one.

6. A: Of these 2 overcoats, which one is expensive? B: The red one is expensive.

7. A: Which floor do you live on? B: I live on the 2nd floor.

8. A: Are Lily's legs long? B: Her legs are very long.

9. A: Are Anna's eyes big or small? B: Her eyes are neither too big nor too small.

10. A: Do you have a headache? B: No, I do not have a headache.

NCC Step 4 Writing Exercises

Ⅰ. Fill in the blanks with the proper words or characters.

> A:那个____红裙子的小姐是你妹妹吗?
>
> B:不是,我妹妹是那个____白帽子的。
>
> A:啊,她个子很____,可是不____。
>
> B:是啊,她身高五呎八吋(一米七三),可是体重一百一十磅(五十公斤),太____了。
>
> A:她的眼睛大大的,腰____ ____的,腿____ ____的。对了,你妹妹的头____怎么样?
>
> B:____黑____长。非常____看。
>
> A:她____眼镜吗?
>
> B:不,她的眼睛是他们班上____好的。

Ⅱ. Please give the antonyms：

	大	长	妈	胖	粗	高	红	黑	姐	哥
Antonym										

215

NCC Step 4　　Writing Exercises

Ⅰ. Fill in the blanks with the proper words or characters.

> A：那個____紅裙子的小姐是你妹妹嗎？
>
> B：不是,我妹妹是那個____白帽子的。
>
> A：啊,她個子很____,可是不____。
>
> B：是啊,她身高五呎八吋(一米七三),可是體重一百一十磅(五十公斤),太____了。
>
> A：她的眼睛大大的,腰____ ____的,腿____ ____的。
> 　　對了,你妹妹的頭____怎麼樣？
>
> B：____黑____長。非常____看。
>
> A：她____眼鏡嗎？
>
> B：不,她的眼睛是他們班上____好的。

Ⅱ. Please give the antonyms：

	大	長	媽	胖	粗	高	紅	黑	姐	哥
Antonym										

NCC Step 4 Special Topic Exercises

的

A. 她是我妹妹的朋友。这本书是我的。
B. 这本书是中文的。
C. 那件衬衫不是新的。
D. 她穿一件很大的衬衫。
E. 我是学汉语的。
F. 穿红裙子的小姐是我妹妹。他喜欢穿红裙子的小姐。

Put the necessary particle "的" into the sentences, and translate the new sentences into English.

1. 王小姐毛衣很好看。
2. 这是一个很好中文课。
3. 小王手最小。
4. 她是昨天十点来我家。
5. 她介绍那个人是她同学。
6. 她鞋子是白。
7. 她有黑色鞋子。
8. 她妈妈是中国人。
9. 她汉语是在中国学。
10. 她上是中文课。

217

NCC Step 4   Special Topic Exercises

的

A. 她是我妹妹的朋友。這本書是我的。
B. 這本書是中文的。
C. 那件襯衫不是新的。
D. 她穿一件很大的襯衫。
E. 我是學漢語的。
F. 穿紅裙子的小姐是我妹妹。他喜歡穿紅裙子的小姐。

Put the necessary particle "的" into the sentences, and translate the new sentences into English.

1. 王小姐毛衣很好看。
2. 這是一個很好中文課。
3. 小王手最小。
4. 她是昨天十點來我家。
5. 她介紹那個人是她同學。
6. 她鞋子是白。
7. 她有黑色鞋子。
8. 她媽媽是中國人。
9. 她漢語是在中國學。
10. 她上是中文課。

NCC Step 4 Reading Comprehension

Based upon the article below, answer the questions or complete the sentences:

Ⅰ. Miss Mimi

> 我叫小毛,今年八岁。我没有哥哥和姐姐,也没有弟弟和妹妹。可是我有一个好朋友,她叫咪咪(mīmi)。我们是在我生日那天认识的。她不高也不矮,非常漂亮。她的一双大眼睛,是灰绿色的。她的耳朵大大的,嘴巴小小的。她穿一件黑毛大衣。她的腿不长也不短,是黑色的。她的腰粗粗的,肚子是白色的。她没有手,可是有四只穿着白袜子的脚。咪咪没有宿舍,她住在我们家。我们都叫她"咪咪小姐"。

1. Mimi is Xiao Mao's _____
    a) pet   b) girl friend   c) older sister

2. Which parts of Mimi are big?
    a) ears and mouth   b) ears and eyes only   c) ears, eyes, and waist

3. Mimi has _____
    a) white tummy   b) white feet   c) white hands

4. Mimi's _____ is not mentioned in the paragraph.
    a) nose   b) legs   c) waist

NCC Step 4   Reading Comprehension

Based upon the article below, answer the questions or complete the sentences:
Ⅰ. Miss Mimi

> 我叫小毛,今年八歲。我沒有哥哥和姐姐,也沒有弟弟和妹妹。可是我有一個好朋友,她叫咪咪(mīmi)。我們是在我生日那天認識的。她不高也不矮,非常漂亮。她的一雙大眼睛,是灰綠色的。她的耳朵大大的,嘴巴小小的。她穿一件黑毛大衣。她的腿不長也不短,是黑色的。她的腰粗粗的,肚子是白色的。她沒有手,可是有四只穿著白襪子的腳。咪咪沒有宿舍,她住在我們家。我們都叫她"咪咪小姐"。

1. Mimi is Xiao Mao's _____
   a) pet   b) girl friend   c) older sister

2. Which parts of Mimi are big?
   a) ears and mouth   b) ears and eyes only   c) ears, eyes, and waist

3. Mimi has _____
   a) white tummy   b) white feet   c) white hands

4. Mimi's _____ is not mentioned in the paragraph.
   a) nose   b) legs   c) waist

NCC Step 4　Special Topic Exercise：Adjectives & Antonyms

Fill out the following form with descriptions suggested in the reading material and Activity 10 in Step 4：

眼睛,嘴巴,耳朵,脖子,肚子,腰,腿,脚,手,头,头发,红,绿,黑,白,蓝,黄,棕,金,灰,灰白,粉红,大,小,粗,细,宽,窄,长,短,胖,瘦,高大,矮小,粗大,细小,瘦高,矮胖,细长,短粗,瘦长,瘦小,漂亮,难看

	很/非常 Adj.	最 Adj.	AA 的	又 A 又 B	不 A 也不 B
Mīmi	黑毛大衣非常漂亮		嘴巴小小的,	灰绿的眼睛又大又亮	腿不长也不短
安娜 Ānnà					
玛丽 Mǎlì					
莉莉 Lìlì					
皮特 Pítè					
马克 Mǎkè					
大卫 Dàwèi					

NCC Step 4   Special Topic Exercise：Adjectives & Antonyms

Fill out the following form with descriptions suggested in the reading material and Activity 10 in Step 4：

眼睛,嘴巴,耳朵,脖子,肚子,腰,腿,腳,手,頭,頭髮,紅,綠,黑,白,藍,黃,棕,金,灰,灰白,粉紅,大,小,粗,細,寬,窄,長,短,胖,瘦,高大,矮小,粗大,細小,瘦高,矮胖,細長,短粗,瘦長,瘦小,漂亮,難看

	很/非常 Adj.	最 Adj.	AA 的	又 A 又 B	不 A 也不 B
Mīmi	黑毛大衣非常漂亮		嘴巴小小的，	灰綠的眼睛又大又亮	腿不長也不短
安娜 Annà					
瑪麗 Mǎlì					
莉莉 Lìlì					
皮特 Pítè					
馬克 Mǎkè					
大衛 Dàwèi					

NCC Step 4 Chapter Exercises

Group: _____ Name: _____

	Characters	Radicals	Phrases	Measure Words	Pinyin (Phrases)	English (Phrases)
1	衬		绿衬/绿衬衫			
2	裤		棕色的裤子			
3	裙		红裙子			
4	鞋		白皮鞋			
5	袜		黄袜子			
6	镜		黑眼镜			
7	帽		灰帽子			
8	发		金头发			
9	耳		小耳朵			
10	腿		长腿			
11	脚		小脚			
12	手		大手			
13	眼		蓝眼睛			
14	脖		短粗的脖子			
15	嘴		大嘴巴			
16	腰		细腰			
17	班		中文班			
18	疼		肚子疼			
19	高		高矮			
20	胖		胖瘦			

223

NCC Step 4 Chapter Exercise

Group: _____ Name: _____

	Characters	Radicals	Phrases	Measure Words	Pinyin (Phrases)	English (Phrases)
1	襯		綠襯衫/綠襯衣			
2	褲		棕色的褲子			
3	裙		紅裙子			
4	鞋		白皮鞋			
5	襪		黃襪子			
6	鏡		黑眼鏡			
7	帽		灰帽子			
8	髮		金頭髮			
9	耳		小耳朵			
10	腿		長腿			
11	腳		小腳			
12	手		大手			
13	眼		藍眼睛			
14	脖		短粗的脖子			
15	嘴		大嘴巴			
16	腰		細腰			
17	班		中文班			
18	疼		肚子疼			
19	高		高矮			
20	胖		胖瘦			

Group:_____ Name:_____

New Century Chinese Book I
Step 5: Classroom & Classes

Homework Assignment List:
Dictation score: _____ + _____ + _____ + _____ = _____
Homework score: _____ + _____ + _____ + _____ = _____

Date	NCC I Workbook	NCC I Textbook	Others

Comments: **Suggestions:**

NCC Step 5　Summary of the Sentence Patterns

Items	Patterns	Sample Sentences
1	"有" sentences expressing existence	他有/没有妹妹。他有没有妹妹？ 教室里有/没有学生。教室里有没有学生？
2	The prepositional phrase 从……来/去, 从 A 到 B 去, 从……点到……点, 在 place, 在 somebody 这/那儿, 跟……一起	那个学生是从美国来的。 我们从大学去小王那儿。 我每天早上从九点到十点上中文课。 我们在大学,不在他那儿吃饭。 他跟我一起学中文。
3	The complement and the particle "得" Verb＋得＋complement（＋object）	小王说得很流利。 他看得完那本书。
4	Degree of complement V＋object＋repeated V＋得＋complement Topicalization	老师今天起得很早。 他睡觉睡得很晚。他睡觉睡得不晚。 他睡觉睡得晚不晚？他睡觉睡得晚吗？ 我汉字写得不好看。 汉字我写得不好看。
5	Pivotal sentences 让、叫、请	老师让我们在家做很多练习； 又叫我们上网（shàng wǎng, get on line）听录音。 我们请老师吃饭。

NCC Step 5　Summary of the Sentence Patterns

Items	Patterns	Sample Sentences
1	"有" sentences expressing existence	他有/沒有妹妹。他有沒有妹妹？ 教室裡有/沒有學生。教室裡有沒有學生？
2	The prepositional phrase 從……來/去，從 A 到 B 去，從……點到……点，在 place，在 somebody 这/那儿，跟……一起	那個學生是從美國來的。 我們從大學去小王那兒。 我每天早上從九點到十點上中文課。 我們在大學，不在他那兒吃飯。 他跟我一起學中文。
3	The complement and the particle "得" Verb＋得＋complement（＋object）	小王説得很流利。 他看得完那本書。
4	Degree of complement V＋object＋repeated V＋得＋complement Topicalization	老師今天起得很早。 他睡覺睡得很晚。他睡覺睡得不晚。 他睡覺睡得晚不晚？他睡覺睡得晚嗎？ 我漢字寫得不好看。 漢字我寫得不好看。
5	Pivotal sentences 讓、叫、請	老師讓我們在家做很多練習； 又叫我們上網（shàng wǎng, get on line）聽錄音。 我們請老師吃飯。

NCC Step 5   Characters

Required Characters

	A	B	C	D	E	F	G	H	I	J
1	把	笔筆	扇	窗	门門	板	教	室	旧舊	里裡
2	书書	新	椅	块塊	张張	枝	桌	共	从從	到
3	授	化	得	历歷	史	每	真	题題	物	理
4	些	校	跟	意	思	难	容	易	喜	欢
5	给	回	答	讲	考	试	作	练	让	写
6	词詞	看	听聽	念唸	准準	备備	流	利	清	楚
7	快	慢	帮幫	助						

Supplementary Characters

	A	B	C	D	E	F	G	H	I	J
1	外	系係	盏盞	灯燈	刷	台臺	空	调調		
2	口	休	政	治	育					
3	图圖	馆館	借	总總	录錄	音	像	影	复復	功

#	Character	Radical	Stroke Order	Example
1	把 bǎ	手 hand	一 † 扌 扌 扩 护 把	一把椅子
2	笔 筆 bǐ	竹 bamboo	ノ ト ケ ケ ケ ケ 竹 竺 笔 / ノ ト ケ ケ ケ 竹 竺 竺 笔 筆	红笔 / 紅筆
3	扇 shàn	羽 feather	、 ⼀ ⼴ ⼾ ⼾ 肩 肩 扇 扇 扇	一扇门 / 一扇門
4	窗 chuāng	穴 cave	、 ⼋ ⼧ ⼧ ⼧ ⼧ 灾 空 窗 窗 窗	窗户
5	门 門 mén		、 ⼀ 门 / 一 ⼆ ⼄ ⼅ 丨 刂 門 門	

#	字	部首	筆順	練習	詞語
6	板 bǎn	木 wood	一 十 才 木 扩 板 板 板	板板板板板板 板板板板板板	黑板
7	教 jiāo, jiào	攴/攵 tap	一 十 土 耂 孝 孝 孝 教 教 教	教教教教教教 教教教教教教	教书 教書
8	室 shì	宀 roof	丶 宀 宀 宀 宀 宰 室 室 室	室室室室室室 室室室室室室	教室
9	旧 舊 jiù	臼 mortar	丨 丨 忄 旧 旧 一 艹 艹 萑 萑 萑 萑 舊 舊 舊	旧旧旧旧旧旧 舊舊舊舊舊舊	旧黑板 舊黑板
10	里 裡 lǐ	衤 clothes	丨 口 日 日 甲 甲 里 丶 ㇇ 衤 衤 衤 初 初 裡 裡 裡	里里里里里里 裡裡裡裡裡裡	教室里 教室裡

233

11	书書 shū	曰 say	㇀ ㇁ 书 书						
			一 ㇁ ㇂ ㇃ 聿 書 書 書 書						
			书	书	书	书	书	书	书	教书 教書
			書	書	書	書	書	書	書	

12	新 xīn	斤 axe	丶 亠 亠 立 立 辛 亲 亲 亲 新 新 新						
			新	新	新	新	新	新		新黑板
			新	新	新	新	新	新		

13	椅 yǐ	木 wood	一 十 才 木 ★ 桁 桁 桁 桁 椅 椅 椅						
			椅	椅	椅	椅	椅	椅	椅	一 ____ 椅子
			椅	椅	椅	椅	椅	椅	椅	

14	块塊 kuài	土 earth	一 十 土 土' 切 块 块						
			一 十 土 土' 切 坦 坦 坥 塊 塊 塊						
			块	块	块	块	块	块	块	一块黑板 一塊黑板
			塊	塊	塊	塊	塊	塊	塊	

15	张張 zhāng	弓 bow	㇀ ㇁ 弓 弓' 弓'' 张 张						
			㇀ ㇁ 弓 弓' 弓'' 弨 弨 張 張 張 張						
			张	张	张	张	张	张	张	一张 一張
			張	張	張	張	張	張	張	

16	枝 zhī	木 wood	一十十才木 枋 枝 枝	
				一枝＿＿＿
17	桌 zhuō	木 wood	丿 卜 卜 占 占 占 卓 桌 桌	
				一＿＿＿桌子
18	共 gòng	八 eight	一 十 廾 艹 共 共	
				一共
19	从 從 cóng	彳 left step	丿 人 从 从 / ノ彳彳彳 彷 径 径 径 從 從	
				从哪儿来？ 從哪兒來？
20	到 dào	刂 knife	一 厶 云 至 至 至 到 到	
				从 A 到 B 從 A 到 B

237

21	授 shòu	手 hand	一 二 キ 扌 扌 扩 扩 护 护 授 授							教授
22	化 huà	匕 ladle	ノ イ 化 化							化学 化學
23	得 dé	彳 left step	ノ ク 彳 彳 彳 彳 彳 徂 得 得 得							觉得 覺得
24	历 歷 lì	止 stop	一 厂 歷 歷 / 一 厂 厂 厈 厈 厤 厤 厤 厤 歷 歷 歷 歷 歷							学历 學歷
25	史 shǐ	口 mouth	丶 口 口 史 史							历史 歷史

#	Character	Radical	Stroke Order	Example
26	每 měi	母 do not	ノ ㇄ 仁 与 每 每 每	每天
27	真 zhēn	目 eye	一 十 广 占 占 肯 首 直 真 真	认真 / 認真
28	题 題 tí	页/頁 page	丨 冂 日 日 旦 早 是 是 是 是 题 题 题 题 / 丨 冂 日 日 旦 早 是 是 是 是 题 题 题 题 題	问题 / 問題
29	物 wù	牛 cow	ノ ㇇ 牛 牛 牛 物 物 物	衣物
30	理 lǐ	王 jade	一 二 干 王 丑 玑 理 理 理 理	物理

241

| 31 | 些 xiē | 二 two | 丨 ト 比 此 此 此 些 些 | | | | | | | 一些 |

| 32 | 校 xiào | 木 wood | 一 十 才 木 术 栌 栌 栌 柺 校 | | | | | | | 学校 / 學校 |

| 33 | 跟 gēn | 足 foot | 丨 ロ ロ 尸 尸 足 足 足 跕 跟 跟 跟 | | | | | | | 我跟你 |

| 34 | 意 yì | 心 heart | 、 亠 亠 立 产 产 咅 音 音 音 意 意 意 | | | | | | | 有意见 / 有意見 |

| 35 | 思 sī | 心 heart | 丨 冂 冃 田 田 思 思 思 | | | | | | | 有意思 |

243

36	难 難 nán	隹 bird	フ ヌ ヌ 对 对 邓 邓 难 难 难 / 一 艹 廿 廿 世 苎 草 草 莫 菓 菓 菓 暵 暵 難 難 難	很难 很難
37	容 róng	穴 cave	` 宀 宀 宀 宀 宀 穴 穴 容 容	不容
38	易 yì	日 sun	丨 口 日 日 旦 旦 易 易	容易
39	喜 xǐ	口 mouth	一 十 士 吉 吉 吉 吉 吉 吉 壴 喜 喜 喜	喜欢 喜歡
40	欢 歡 huān	欠 owe	フ ヌ ヌ 对 欢 欢 / 一 艹 艹 艹 艹 艹 艹 艹 艹 艹 芇 莑 莑 莑 莑 歡 歡 歡	喜欢 喜歡

245

41	给 給 gěi	纟/糸 silk	乙幺幺纟纠纶给给给						
			乙幺幺纟纠纶给给给给						
			给	给	给	给	给	给	给人 給人
			给	给	给	给	给	给	

42	回 huí	囗 enclosure	丨冂冂冋冋回						
			回	回	回	回	回	回	回家
			回	回	回	回	回	回	

43	答 dá	竹 bamboo	丿丿竹竹竹竹竹筚筚答答答						
			答	答	答	答	答	答	回答
			答	答	答	答	答	答	

44	讲 講 jiǎng	讠/言 word	丶讠讠讠讲讲						
			丶亠亠言言言言言詝譁譁講講講講						
			讲	讲	讲	讲	讲	讲	讲语法 講語法
			講	講	講	講	講	講	

45	考 kǎo	耂 old	一十土耂耂考						
			考	考	考	考	考	考	考上
			考	考	考	考	考	考	

46	试 試 shì	讠/言 word	`丶 讠 计 计 计 试 试 试` `丶 一 二 亖 言 言 言 言 訁 訐 試 試`	考试 考試
47	作 zuò	亻 people	`丿 亻 亻 亻 竹 作 作`	作练习 作練習
48	练 練 liàn	纟/糹 silk	`乙 纟 纟 纟 纴 练 练 练` `乙 纟 纟 纟 糹 糹 紅 紅 紳 紳 練 練 練`	练习 練習
49	让 讓 ràng	讠/言 word	`丶 讠 计 计 让` `丶 一 二 亖 言 言 言 訁 訐 諮 讓 讓 讓 讓 讓 讓 讓`	A 让 B 作…… A 讓 B 作……
50	写 寫 xiě	宀 roof	`丶 冖 冖 写 写` `丶 冖 宀 宀 宀 宁 宁 宆 寫 寫 寫 寫 寫`	写书 寫書

249

#	Character	Radical	Stroke Order	Example
51	词 詞 cí	讠/言 word	丶 讠 讠 词 词 词 词 丶 二 三 言 言 言 訂 詞 詞 詞 詞	生词 生詞
52	看 kàn	目 eye	一 二 三 手 禾 看 看 看 看	看书 看書
53	听 聽 tīng	耳 ear	丶 丨 口 叮 叮 听 听 一 丁 丁 丁 耳 耳 耳 聊 聊 聊 聊 聊 聽 聽 聽 聽	听力 聽力
54	念 唸 niàn	心 heart	丿 人 亼 今 念 念 念 丨 口 口 叮 叮 哈 哈 唸 唸 唸	念课文 唸課文
55	准 準 zhǔn	氵 water	丶 冫 冫 冫 汁 汁 汁 准 准 丶 冫 冫 氵 汁 汁 汁 汁 淮 淮 準	钟不准 鐘不準

#	字	部首	笔顺	练习	词语
56	备 備 bèi	亻 people	ノク夂冬各各备备 ノイ仁仁仕併併併備備備	备备备备备备 備備備備備備	准备 準備
57	流 liú	氵 water	丶丶氵氵浐浐浐浐流流	流流流流流流 流流流流流流	从A流到B 從A流到B
58	利 lì	刂 knife	ノ二千禾禾利利	利利利利利利 利利利利利利	流利
59	清 qīng	氵 water	丶丶氵氵氵清清清清清	清清清清清清 清清清清清清	很清
60	楚 chǔ	木 wood	一十才木木村村林林梺梺楚楚	楚楚楚楚楚楚 楚楚楚楚楚楚	清楚

253

#	Character	Radical	Stroke Order	Examples
61	快 kuài	忄 heart	丶丶忄忄忄快快	不快
62	慢 màn	忄 heart	丶丶忄忄忄忄忄慢慢慢慢慢慢	快慢
63	帮 幫 bāng	巾 napkin	一三丰邦邦帮帮 / 一十士圭圭圭圭圭封封封封幫幫幫	帮人 幫人
64	助 zhù		丨冂冃且助助	帮助 幫助

NCC Step 5 Listening Comprehension Exercises

I. 1) Write down the following questions in *pinyin*;
   2) Answer the questions in <u>characters</u> according to the chart in Activity 5 (p. 128).

1. Q: _____

   A: _____

2. Q: _____

   A: _____

3. Q: _____

   A: _____

II. 1) Write down the questions in <u>English</u>;
    2) Answer the questions in <u>characters</u> based upon your situation.

1. Q: _____

   A: _____

2. Q: _____

   A: _____

3. Q: _____

   A: _____

4. Q: _____

   A: _____

NCC Step 5 Listening Comprehension Test

Instruction: Based on the paragraph/dialogue your heard, answer the following T/F questions. Each piece will be read twice.

Paragraph
1. _____ Xiao Wang is an exchange student from China.
2. _____ Xiao Wang has class from 10:00 to 11:00 a.m. everyday.
3. _____ Xiao Wang speaks Chinese fluently.
4. _____ xiao Wang likes to read books in the dormitory.
5. _____ Xiao Wang often does his homework at the library.

Dialogue
1. _____ Xiao Wang is taking 5 classes this term.
2. _____ Xiao Wang is NOT taking politics this term.
3. _____ Xiao Wang doesn't like English Literature class, because it is too hard.
4. _____ Xiao Wang likes Prof. Li's class because she is beautiful.
5. _____ Prof. Li is from England.

NCC Step 5 Character Exercises

I. Radical recognition: Find the characters with the same radicals and fill in the blanks:

笔/筆,扇,窗,张/張,图/圖,块/塊,教,室,桌,椅,得,理,回,答,讲/講,考,试/試,看,让/讓,常,帮/幫,助,对/對,欢/歡,数/數,体/體

		A	B	C	D
1	羽				
2	穴				
3	口				
4	力				
5	弓				
6	目				
7	讠/言				
8	寸				
9	竹				
10	文				
11	欠				
12	木				
13	王				
14	乡				
15	巾				
16	彳				
17	土				
18	骨				

II. Tone differentiation: Give the *pinyin* equivalent to each character.

1	ba	把____	巴____	爸____	
2	bi	笔/筆____	鼻____		
3	shan	扇____	衫____		
4	men	们/們____	门/門____		
5	ban	板____	班____		
6	jiao	教____	脚/腳____	叫____	觉/覺____
7	li	理____	李____	利____	丽/麗____
8	shu	书/書____	数/數____		
9	shi	试/試____	室____	史____	师/師____
10	yi	椅____	衣____		
11	si	思____	四____		
12	wu	物____	五____		
13	xiao	校____	小____		
14	da	答____	大____		
15	qing	清____	请/請____		
16	zhi	枝____	址____	只/隻____	纸/紙____
17	xie	些____	谢/謝____	鞋____	写/寫____
18	jing	睛____	京____		

Ⅲ. Character differentiation: Give the equivalent character to each phrase.

	Shared Sounds	Fill in the Blanks with Different Characters		
1	jiào	他____大中	____授	睡____
2	shì	我　　老师 我____老師	教____	考____
3	lǐ	物____	家____	姓____
4	kuài	一____	____慢	
5	dé	说　　快 說____快	语____ 語____	
6	měi	国 國 ____	____天	
7	lì	____史	流____	
8	nán	____人	很____	
9	yì	____思	容____	
10	liú	____利	学____ 學____	姓____
11	shòu	胖____	教____	
12	zhù	帮____ 幫____	____址	

265

Ⅳ. Fill in the blanks with the appropriate measure words:

1	两____课	7	两____窗户
2	两____教授	8	两____地图
3	两____黑板	9	两____灯
4	两____椅子	10	两____空调机
5	两____桌子	11	两____笔
6	两____书	12	两____问题

Ⅴ. Distinguish similar characters: For each character, give the correct *pinyin* equivalent in the shaded column:

1	穿		穿	
2	给		绍	
3	清		请	
4	学		觉	
5	回		问	
6	板		饭	
7	教		数	
8	跟		很	
9	欢		难	

Ⅳ. Fill in the blanks with the appropriate measure words:

1	兩____課		7	兩____窗戶	
2	兩____教授		8	兩____地圖	
3	兩____黑板		9	兩____燈	
4	兩____椅子		10	兩____空調機	
5	兩____桌子		11	兩____筆	
6	兩____書		12	兩____問題	

Ⅴ. Distinguish similar characters: For each character, give the correct *pinyin* equivalent in the shaded column:

1	穿		穿	
2	給		紹	
3	清		請	
4	學		覺	
5	回		問	
6	板		飯	
7	教		數	
8	跟		很	
9	歡		難	

NCC Step 5 Translation Exercises

1. There are many desks in the dormitory.

2. His sister attends English class from 9:00 to 9:50 everyday.

3. We go to Mrs. Wang's place to ask questions.

4. Xiao Ding often studies English with Xiao Chen.

5. Do you read fast or slowly?

6. Our teacher explains the grammar clearly.

7. My friend writes characters extremely beautiful (*using topicalization*).

8. My mom asks me to wear that white shirt.

9. Mr. Fang asks Miss Wang to answer two questions.

10. His father asks him to get up at seven every morning.

NCC Step 5　Writing Exercises

Fill in the blanks with the proper words or <u>characters</u>.

1. A: 你们的教室里都有什么？
   B: 有八_____桌子，八_____椅子，两_____窗户，一_____黑板和一_____空调机。
   A: 有没有地图？
   B: 有一_____中国地图。
   A: 空调机是不是_____的？
   B: 不，是旧的。

2. A: 你们班上一_____有多少学生？
   B: 有十八_____学生。
   A: 你们的老师_____是美国人吗？
   B: _____是。一个是英国人，两个是美国人。

3. A: 这个学期你上几_____课？
   B: 五_____。
   A: 你觉得这些课都很_____吗？
   B: 不，文学和政治都很容_____。
   A: 你最喜_____什么课？
   B: 历_____课，数_____课和物_____课。

271

NCC Step 5　Writing Exercises

Fill in the blanks with the proper words or <u>characters</u>.

1. A:你們的教室裡都有甚麼?
   B:有八_____桌子,八_____椅子,兩_____窗戶,一_____黑板和一_____空調機。
   A:有沒有地圖?
   B:有一_____中國地圖。
   A:空調機是不是_____的?
   B:不,是舊的。

2. A:你們班上一_____有多少學生?
   B:有十八_____學生。
   A:你們的老師_____是美國人嗎?
   B:_____是。一個是英國人,兩個是美國人。

3. A:這個學期你上幾_____課?
   B:五_____。
   A:你覺得這些課都很_____嗎?
   B:不,文學和政治都很容_____。
   A:你最喜_____甚麼課?
   B:歷_____課,數_____課和物_____課。

Please give the proper complements to describe the following activities:

问问题 问得	作练习 作得	念课文 念得	讲语法 讲得	考试 考得	写汉字 写得
問問題 問得	作練習 作得	唸課文 唸得	講語法 講得	考試 考得	寫漢字 寫得

NCC Step 5 Special Topic Exercises

得

Please make sentences based upon the phrases given:

	Phrases	Pinyin	English	多/少,好/不好,快/慢,难/容易,认真/不认真,对/不对,漂亮/难看,流利/不流利,清楚/不清楚 小王看中文书看得非常多。/中文书小王看得非常多。
eg.	看中文书	kàn Zhōngwén shū	read Chinese books	
1	说汉语			
2	写汉字			
3	讲语法			
4	问问题			
5	回答问题			
6	做功课			
7	做练习			
8	听录音			
9	念课文			
10	考试			
11	复习课文			

NCC Step 5 Special Topic Exercises

Please make sentences based upon the phrases given:

得

多/少,好/不好,快/慢,難/容易,認真/不認真,對/不對,漂亮/難看,流利/不流利,清楚/不清楚

小王看中文書看得非常多。／中文書小王看得非常多。

	Phrases	Pinyin	English	
eg.	看中文書	kàn Zhōngwén shū	read Chinese books	
1	說漢語			
2	寫漢字			
3	講語法			
4	問問題			
5	回答問題			
6	做功課			
7	做練習			
8	聽錄音			
9	唸課文			
10	考試			
11	復習課文			

NCC Step 5 Chapter Exercises

Group: _____ Name: _____

	Characters	Radicals	Phrases	Pinyin	English	Sentences
1	窗		一扇窗户/门			
2	板		一（ ）黑板			
3	椅		一（ ）椅子			
4	室		一（ ）教室			
5	书		一（ ）新书			
6	笔		一（ ）旧笔			
7	图		一（ ）地图			
8	化		一（ ）化学课			
9	教		一（ ）数学教授			
10	期		两（ ）学期			
11	考		考试			
12	难		难题			
13	易		容易			
14	欢		喜欢			
15	真		认真			
16	答		回答问题			
17	流		念得流利			
18	清		看得清楚			
19	帮		帮助			
20	准		准备			

NCC Step 5 Chapter Exercises

Group: _____ Name: _____

	Characters	Radicals	Phrases	*Pinyin*	English	Sentences
1	窗		一扇窗戶/門			
2	板		一（　）黑板			
3	椅		一（　）椅子			
4	室		一（　）教室			
5	書		一（　）新書			
6	筆		一（　）舊筆			
7	圖		一（　）地圖			
8	化		一（　）化學課			
9	數		一（　）數學教授			
10	期		兩（　）學期			
11	考		考試			
12	難		難題			
13	易		容易			
14	歡		喜歡			
15	真		認真			
16	答		回答問題			
17	流		念得流利			
18	清		看得清楚			
19	幫		幫助			
20	準		準備			

Guided Composition: My Best Friend

Based on the theme mentioned and questions asked, write a 3-paragraph essay about your best friend. This page is your rough draft. You may fill it out in English/Chinese and turn it in with your final copy of the essay. Please write your essay on the assigned paper. The essay will be graded based upon: Vocabulary, grammar, creativity, and punctuation.

Title: 我的好朋友	
一	谁是你的好朋友？她/他叫什么名字？是哪国人？她/他家有几个人？都是谁？ 誰是你的好朋友？她/他叫甚麼名字？是哪國人？她/他家有幾個人？都是誰？
1	
2	
3	
3	
4	
5	
6	
7	
二	她/他今年多大？是学生吗？在哪儿学习？学习什么？上几门课？说什么语言？谁是她/他的老师？ 她/他今年多大？是學生嗎？在哪兒學習？學習甚麼？上幾門課？説甚麼語言？誰是她/他的老師？
1	
2	

3	
3	
4	
5	
6	
7	

三	她/他住在哪儿？她/他的电话号码是多少？她/他忙不忙？有男/女朋友吗？ 她/他住在哪兒？她/他的電話號碼是多少？她/他忙不忙？有男/女朋友嗎？
1	
2	
3	
3	
4	
5	
6	
7	

comments	1.
	2.

Group:_____ Name:_____

我 的 好 朋 友

Class & Self-Evaluation

In order to help us improve our study, please complete this survey form (circle one number). Your time and effort spent in giving us comments and suggestions are greatly appreciated.

	Categories		From the least (1) to the most (5)	Your comments & Suggestions
1	Textbook (NCC)	a. Functions & topics selected b. Character version format c. Activities in the text d. Grammar notes	1 2 3 4 5 1 2 3 4 5 1 2 3 4 5 1 2 3 4 5	
2	Supplements:	a. Monthly calendar b. Daily schedule c. Content of each step or unit d. Web site listening e. Visual aids, flash cards	1 2 3 4 5 1 2 3 4 5 1 2 3 4 5 1 2 3 4 5 1 2 3 4 5	
3	Homework:	a. Listening comprehension on web b. Character writing worksheet c. Grammar exercises d. In-class grammar or review worksheet	1 2 3 4 5 1 2 3 4 5 1 2 3 4 5 1 2 3 4 5	
4	In Class. Activities	a. Group work b. Pair practice, pair dialogue, interview c. Individual work	1 2 3 4 5 1 2 3 4 5 1 2 3 4 5	
5	Evaluation & Grading	a. Attendance b. Daily dictation c. Quizzes d. Listening comprehension test e. Speaking test f. Skit g. Analyzing the article and essay	1 2 3 4 5 1 2 3 4 5 1 2 3 4 5 1 2 3 4 5 1 2 3 4 5 1 2 3 4 5 1 2 3 4 5	
6	Others	a. Format & objective of the class b. Interaction (teacher-students) c. Interaction (students-students) d. Office hour/special help e. Classroom order & setting	1 2 3 4 5 1 2 3 4 5 1 2 3 4 5 1 2 3 4 5 1 2 3 4 5	

Appendix: Tapescripts and Keys

Pinyin Exercises

Please listen to the recording/on-line and do the following exercises.

Ⅰ. Tone Recognition (1): Circle the ones with the tones that you hear.

	1st(ˉ)	2nd(ˊ)	3rd(ˇ)	4th(ˋ)
1	mā			
2				dì
3			tǔ	
4		liú		
5				gùn
6			jǔ	
7		zhí		
8	sōng			
9		chén		
10			rǎn	

Tone Recognition (2): Circle the ones with the correct tones that you hear.

1		kān jiā
2	lǎoshī	
3		guànxīn
4	piàoliàng	
5	rènshi	

II. Initial Recognition: Circle the ones with the initials that you hear.

1	bǎ		
2		kàn	
3			gé
4	xiǎng		
5		diào	
6	qín		
7		kuān	
8	zhēn		
9		zuì	
10			chóu

III. Final Recognition: Circle the ones with the finals that you hear.

1	xiū	
2	qián	
3	shì	
4		duǒ
5	yuán	
6		pīn
7	mǒ	
8		nù
9	yóu	
10	liù	

IV. Spelling Rules (1): Circle the *pinyin* with the correct spelling.

1	jūn	
2		yìng
3	qióng	
4	niú	
5		duì
6	wǒ	
7	qù	
8	yáng	
9		yún
10	pō	

Spelling Rules (2): Mark the tones you hear on the correct positions.

1	jīngyàn
2	chúnjiǔ
3	quánwēi
4	biànle
5	shěnglüè

Spelling Rules (3): Write down the *pinyin* equivalents.

1	Zhōngguó
2	shānshuǐ
3	qiánchéng
4	fóguāngyuán
5	xìn kǒu kāi hé

NCC Step 1 Pronunciation Exercises

I. Tone discrimination: Circle the right tones you hear.

	A	B		A	B
1	wèi		2		nǐ
3	wǒ		4		xìng
5		péng	6	lái	
7	guì		8		xiān
9		qǐng wèn	10	bù	
11		dīng	12		qī
13	máng		14		shū
15	shǒu		16		zhàn
17		hěn	18	chén	
19	duì		20	dōu	

II. Sound discrimination: Circle the *pinyin* you hear.

	A	B		A	B
1	zhè		2		wǒ
3	nǐ		4		shì
5	hǎo		6		nín
7	lái		8	jièshào	
9	xìng		10	xiǎo	
11		péng	12		shén
13		wèn	14	xiān	
15		míngzi	16	dé	
17		nán	18	hàn	
19	yǒu		20	qǐ	
21	fāng		22	wáng	
23		chén	24	xiè	
25	yě		26		hěn
27		dōu	28	wǎn	
29		máng	30	shàng	
31	shàngkè		32		ān
33	yǒu		34	zuò	
35		zhàn	36	qù	
37	shǒu		38	zǎo	
39		qī	40	qǐng	

NCC Step 1 Listening Comprehension Exercises

I. 1) Write down the following questions in *pinyin* or Englsih;
   2) Answer each questions in *pinyin*.

1. A: Qǐngwèn, nín guìxìng?
   B: wǒ xìng ___Chi___, wǒ jiào ___Carol Chi___

2. A: Nǐ de Hànyǔ lǎoshī xìng shénme? Jiào shénme?
   B: Tā xìng ___Wu___, jiào ~~老~~ ___Wu. Xiaozhou___

3. A: Nǐ rènshi Fāng Jiè ma?
   B: Wǒ bú rènshi Fāng Jiè.

4. A: Qǐngwèn, Mǎ xiǎojiě jiào shénme míngzi?
   B: Tā jiào Mǎ Xiǎohóng.

5. A: Qǐngwèn, nǐ de nánpéngyou xìng shénme?
   B: Tā xìng ___Duong___.

6. A: Nín zǎo.
   B: Nín zǎo.

7. A: Nǐ máng ma?
   B: Wǒ hěn máng.
   A: Fāng xiānsheng ne?
   B: Tā yě hěn máng.

NCC Step 1 Listening Comprehension Test

Instruction: Based upon the following dialogues between a man and a woman, determine whether the statements are "True" or "False". Each dialogue will be read twice.

Ⅰ. 丁：请问，先生，您贵姓？
　　丁：請問，先生，您貴姓？
　　王：我姓王，叫大中，你呢？
　　王：我姓王，叫大中，你呢？
　　丁：我叫丁美美。
　　丁：我叫丁美美。
　　王：你认识陈小姐吗？
　　王：你認識陳小姐嗎？
　　丁：不认识。她是谁？
　　丁：不認識。她是誰？
　　王：她是我的汉语老师，也是我的女朋友。
　　王：她是我的漢語老師，也是我的女朋友。

Ⅱ. 皮特：早，杨老师！
　　皮特：早，楊老師！
　　老师：早，皮特！你忙吗？
　　老師：早，皮特！你忙嗎？
　　皮特：不很忙，老师，您呢？
　　皮特：不很忙，老師，您呢？
　　老师：很忙，很忙。
　　老師：很忙，很忙。
　　皮特：杨老师，您认识我的女朋友吗？
　　皮特：楊老師，您認識我的女朋友嗎？
　　老师：对不起，不认识。
　　老師：對不起，不認識。
　　皮特：来，我介绍一下，这位是我的女朋友玛丽，这位是杨老师。
　　皮特：來，我介紹一下，這位是我的女朋友瑪麗，這位是楊老師。

Keys：
　　Dialogue Ⅰ：1. F　2. F　3. T　4. T
　　Dialogue Ⅱ：1. F　2. F　3. T　4. F

NCC Step 2 Pronunciation Exercises

I. Tone discrimination: Circle the right tones you hear.

	A	B		A	B
1	líng		2	èr	
3		yī	4	liù	
5	liǎng		6	děng	
7	xiàn		8		diàn
9	kè		10		chà
11	fàn		12		xiè
13	běi		14	qián	
15	yǒu		16	fēicháng	
17	nǐ hǎo		18	nǐ ne	
19	qíngtiān		20		jièshào

II. Sound discrimination: Circle the *pinyin* you hear.

	A	B		A	B
1	qī		2	chéng	
3		jiǎn	4	diǎn	
5		chuáng	6	chī	
7	guǎng		8	guī	
9	jiā		10		fēijī
11	qián		12	xiāng	
13		rè	14	jīn	
15		shān	16	chà	
17	nián		18	xiàwǔ	
19		wǎnshang	20	rì	
21	liǎng		22	děngyú	

293

NCC Step 2　Listening Comprehension Exercises

Ⅰ. (Activity Three) Write down the following mathematics questions in English and give the answers.
  1. 4＋3＝7　 2. 15＋81＝96
  3. 29－17＝12　 4. 115－5＝110
  5. 5×8＝40　 6. 9×7＝63

Ⅱ. (Activity Four) Translate the following dialogues into English.
  1. A:王小姐,请问现在几点钟?　 (A: Miss Wang, May I ask what time is it?)
   A:王小姐,請問現在幾點鐘?
   B:现在差一刻三点。   (B: It is 2:45)
   B:現在差一刻三點。
  2. A:请问谢先生,现在几点钟? (A: Mr. Xie, what time is it now?)
   A:請問謝先生,現在幾點鐘?
   B:现在十点十分。   (B: It is 10:10)
   B:現在十點十分。
  3. A:马克,现在几点钟?   (A: What time is it now, Mark?)
   A:馬克,現在幾點鐘?
   B:现在下午四点三十分。   (B: It is 4:30 p.m. now)
   B:現在下午四點三十分。

Ⅲ. (Activity Five) 1) Write down the following questions in English.　2) Based on the brief daily schedule on p. 35 or p. 48-49 (character version), answer the questions in *pinyin*.
  1. Q:方介晚上七点〇五分还是七点一刻吃饭?
    方介晚上七點〇五分還是七點一刻吃飯?
   (Does Fang Jie have dinner at 7:05 or 7:15 p.m.?)
   A: Fāng Jiè wǎnshang qī diǎn líng wǔ fēn chīfàn.
  2. Q:是安娜还是皮特中午十二点三十五分吃饭?
    是安娜還是皮特中午十二點三十五分吃飯?
   (Does Anna or Peter have lunch at 12:35?)
   A: Shì Pítè zhōngwǔ shí'èr diǎn sānshíwǔ fēn chīfàn.
  3. Q:玛丽下午四点一刻还是四点三刻下课?
    瑪麗下午四點一刻還是四點三刻下課?
   (Does Mary finish class at 4:15 p.m. or 4:45 p.m.?)
   A: Mǎlì xiàwǔ sì diǎn sān kè xiàkè.

Ⅳ. (Activity Seven) 1) Write down the following questions in *pinyin* or English. 2) Based on the flight schedule on p. 36 or p. 50-51 (character version), answer the questions in *pinyin*.
1. Q: Běijīng dào Niǔyuē de fēijī shì xiàwǔ liǎng diǎn èrshí fēn qǐfēi ma?
   A: Běijīng dào Niǔyuē de fēijī shì xiàwǔ liǎng diǎn èrshí fēn qǐfēi.
2. Q: Xī'ān dào Běijīng de fēijī jǐ diǎn dào?
   A: Xī'ān dào Běijīng de fēijī wǎnshang qī diǎn sānshíjiǔ fēn dào.
3. Q: Guǎngzhōu dào běijīng de fēijī xiàwǔ liǎng diǎn bàn háishi sì diǎn èrshíwǔ fēn dào?
   A: Guǎngzhōu dào běijīng de fēijī xiàwǔ sì diǎn èrshíwǔ fēn dào.

Ⅴ. (Activity Eleven) 1) Write down the following dialogues in *pinyin*.
   2) Translate them into English.
A: Shànghǎi qīyuè de tiānqi zěnmeyàng?
   (How is the weather in Shanghai in July?)
B: Fēicháng rè.
   (Very hot.)
A: Wǔyuè ne?
   (How about May?)
B: Bù lěng yě bú rè.
   (Neither cold nor hot.)

NCC Step 2 Listening Comprehension Test

Instruction: Based upon the following dialogues between a man and a woman, determine whether the statements are "True" or "False". Each dialogue will be read twice.

Ⅰ. M:上个星期是我的生日。
   M:上個星期是我的生日。
   W:是吗？您的生日是几月几号？
   W:是嗎？您的生日是幾月幾號？
   M:我的生日是七月二十日。
   M:我的生日是七月二十日。
   W:今年您的生日是星期几？
   W:今年您的生日是星期幾？
   M:星期五。
   M:星期五。
   W:您是一九六八年还是一九六九年生的？
   W:您是一九六八年還是一九六九年生的？
   M:六八年,你呢？
   M:六八年,你呢？
   W:六〇年。
   W:六〇年。

Ⅱ. A:北京十月的天气很冷还是很热？
   A:北京十月的天氣很冷還是很熱？
   B:不冷也不热。
   B:不冷也不熱。
   A:十一月呢？
   A:十一月呢？
   B:非常冷。洛杉矶十一月的天气怎么样？
   B:非常冷。洛杉磯十一月的天氣怎麼樣？
   A:有一点儿冷。
   A:有一點兒冷。

Ⅲ. A:请问,北京到洛杉矶的第123号航班几点起飞?
   A:請問,北京到洛杉磯的第123號航班幾點起飛?
   B:下午两点半。
   B:下午兩點半。
   A:小姐,您的表现在几点?
   A:小姐,您的錶現在幾點?
   B:差一刻两点。
   B:差一刻兩點。
   A:谢谢你。
   A:謝謝你。
   B:不客气。
   B:不客氣。

Keys:
   DialogueⅠ: 1. T 2. F 3. T 4. F
   DialogueⅡ: 1. T 2. F 3. F
   DialogueⅢ: 1. F 2. T 3. F

NCC Step 3 Listening Comprehension Exercises

Ⅰ. (After Activity One) Write down the following dialogues in *pinyin*.

1. A：Fǎguó rén shuō Yīngyǔ háishi Rìyǔ?
   B：Fǎguó rén bù shuō Yīngyǔ yě bù shuō Rìyǔ.
2. A：Xiǎo Wáng shuō Hànyǔ ma?
   B：Xiǎo Wáng shuō Yīngyǔ yě shuō Hànyǔ.
3. A：Zhōngguó rén shuō bu shuō Yīngyǔ?
   B：Zhōngguó rén shuō Hànyǔ, bù shuō Yīngyǔ.

Ⅱ. Based upon Activity 8 (p. 72 or p. 85):
   1) Write down the questions in *pinyin*.
   2) Answer the questions in characters.

1. Q：Zhè shì shéi de shēnfènzhèng?
   A：这是王贵生的身份证。
   A：這是王貴生的身份證。
2. Q：Shēnfènzhèng de hàomǎ shì duōshao?
   A：身份证的号码是四五二五二一七三〇六二四〇〇七。
   A：身份证的號碼是四五二五二一七三〇六二四〇〇七。
3. Q：Zhè ge rén zhù zài nǎr?
   A：这个人住在北京市学院路一八九号。
   A：這個人住在北京市學院路一八九號。
4. A：Zhè ge rén shì nǎ nián nǎ yuè nǎ rì chūshēng de?
   A：这个人是一九七三年六月二十四日出生的。
   A：這個人是一九七三年六月二十四日出生的。
5. Q：Zhè ge rén shì zài nǎr chūshēng de?
   A：这个人是在北京出生的。
   A：这个人是在北京出生的。

NCC Step 3 Listening Comprehension Test

Instruction: Based upon the following dialogues between a man and a woman, determine whether the statements are "True" or "False". Each dialogue will be read twice.

I. M:那是谁?
   M:那是誰?
   W:那是我同学田中先生。
   W:那是我同學田中先生。
   M:他是不是日本人?
   M:他是不是日本人?
   W:是。他说英语、汉语,可是不说日语。
   W:是。他說英語、漢語,可是不説日語。
   M:他今年多大?
   M:他今年多大?
   W:他今年二十一岁。
   W:他今年二十一歲。

II. M:你住在哪儿?
    M:你住在哪兒?
    W:我住在学生宿舍。
    W:我住在學生宿舍。
    M:你住多少号?
    M:你住多少號?
    W:五层五〇二号,你呢?
    W:五層五〇二號,你呢?
    M:我不住在宿舍,我住在家。
    M:我不住在宿舍,我住在家。
    W:你家的电话号码是多少?
    W:你家的電話號碼是多少?
    M:我家的電話號碼是:(949)873-8864。
    M:我家的电话号码是:(949)873-8864。

Ⅲ. M：王小姐，您的汉语非常好，你是在哪儿学的？
　　M：王小姐，您的漢語非常好，你是在哪兒學的？
　　W：我是在北京学的，你呢，丁先生？
　　W：我是在北京學的，你呢，丁先生？
　　M：我是在美国洛杉矶学的。
　　M：我是在美國洛杉磯學的。
　　W：你是学什么的？
　　W：你是學甚麽的？
　　M：我、我太太都学习法语。
　　M：我、我太太都學習法語。
　　W：现在你们的法语怎么样？
　　W：現在你們的法語怎麽樣？
　　M：我太太的法语非常好，可是我的差一点儿。
　　M：我太太的法語非常好，可是我的差一點兒。

Keys：
　　Dialogue Ⅰ：1. F　2. F　3. F
　　Dialogue Ⅱ：1. F　2. T　3. F
　　Dialogue Ⅲ：1. T　2. F　3. F　4. T

NCC Step 4　Listening Comprehension Exercises

Ⅰ. Based upon Activity 1, 1)Write down the following questions in *pinyin*. 2)Answer the questions in <u>characters</u> according to the chart in Activity 1 (p. 91 or p. 102).

1. Q: Èr hào shì bái de háishi huáng de?
   A:二号是黄的。
   A:二號是黄的。
2. Q: Qī hào shì huī de háishi hēi de?
   A:都不是,七号是紫的。
   A:都不是,七號是紫的。
3. Q: Wǔ hào shì bái de ma?
   A:对,五号是白的。
   A:對,五號是白的。
4. Q: Sān hào shì shénme yánsè de?
   A:三号是绿的。
   A:三號是綠的。

Ⅱ. Based upon Activity 6, 1)Write down the questions in *pinyin*. 2)Answer the questions in <u>characters</u> according to the picture in Activity 6 (p. 96 or 109).

1. Q: Tā de bízi dà háishi xiǎo?
   A:他的鼻子非常大。
   A:他的鼻子非常大。
2. Q: Tā de zuǐba bú tài dà, shì ma?
   A:对,他的嘴巴不太大。
   A:對,他的嘴巴不太大。
3. Q: Tā de ěrduo dà bu dà?
   A:他的耳朵非常小。
   A:他的耳朵非常小。
4. Q: Tā de yāo shì xì de háishi cū de?
   A:他的腰不粗也不细。
   A:他的腰不粗也不細。

301

NCC Step 4　Listening Comprehension Test

Instruction: Based upon the following dialogues between a man and a woman, determine whether the statements are "True" or "False". Each dialogue will be read twice.

Ⅰ. 男:这件白衬衫怎么样?
　　男:這件白襯衫怎麼樣?
　　女:不好,有一点儿长。
　　女:不好,有一點兒長。
　　男:那件红色的呢?
　　男:那件紅色的呢?
　　女:那件不长也不短,可是太贵了。
　　女:那件不長也不短,可是太貴了。

Ⅱ. 女:小王,你现在有女朋友吗?
　　女:小王,你現在有女朋友嗎?
　　男:没有,你给我介绍一个。
　　男:沒有,你給我介紹一個。
　　女:好啊,那个穿红裙子的小姐怎么样?
　　女:好啊,那個穿紅裙子的小姐怎麼樣?
　　男:她一点儿也不漂亮。眼睛太小,嘴巴太大,还戴着一副大眼镜。
　　男:她一點兒也不漂亮。眼睛太小,嘴巴太大,還戴著一副大眼鏡。
　　女:可是,她是我们汉语班上学习最好的学生。
　　女:可是,她是我們漢語班上學習最好的學生。
　　男:可是我喜欢漂亮的。
　　男:可是我喜歡漂亮的。

Ⅲ. 男:王小姐,您请坐。您哪儿疼啊? 腰疼不疼啊? 头呢?
　　男:王小姐,您請坐。您哪兒疼啊? 腰疼不疼啊? 頭呢?
　　女:都不疼。
　　女:都不疼。
　　男:腿呢?
　　男:腿呢?

女：也不疼，可是我的肚子现在很疼很疼。
女：也不疼，可是我的肚子現在很疼很疼。

Ⅳ. 男：你们汉语班上谁最高？
男：你們漢語班上誰最高？
女：小王最高。可是他的腿不长。
女：小王最高。可是他的腿不長。
男：他的脚大不大？
男：他的腳大不大？
女：他的脚非常大，他穿十三号的球鞋，可是他今年才十二岁。
女：他的腳非常大，他穿十三號的球鞋，可是他今年才十二歲。

Keys：
 Dialogue Ⅰ：1. F 2. T 3. T
 Dialogue Ⅱ：1. T 2. F 3. T
 Dialogue Ⅲ：1. F 2. T 3. F
 Dialogue Ⅳ：1. T 2. F 3. F

NCC Step 5 Listening Comprehension Exercises

Ⅰ. 1) Write down the following questions in *pinyin*.
   2) Answer the questions in <u>characters</u> according to the chart in Activity 5 (p. 128).

1. Q: Hǎilún xīngqīsān dōu yǒu shénme kè?
   A: 她星期三有文学课,历史课和法语课。
   A: 她星期三有文學課,歷史課和法語課。

2. Q: Lìshǐ kè de lǎoshī shì shéi?
   A: 是金教授。
   A: 是金教授。

3. Q: Hǎilún nǎ jǐ tiān yǒu tǐyù kè?
   A: 她星期二和星期四有体育课。
   A: 她星期二和星期四有體育課。

Ⅱ. 1) Write down the questions in <u>English</u>.
   2) Answer the questions in <u>characters</u> based upon your situation.

1. Q: How many classes do you take this semester?
   这个学期你上几门课?
   這個學期你上幾門課?
   A: 这个学期我上_____门课。
   A: 這個學期我上_____門課。

2. Q: What time do you go to class (at school) everyday?
   你每天几点到学院上课?
   你每天幾點到學院上課?
   A: 我每天_____点(去学院)上课。
   A: 我每天_____點(去學院)上課。

3. Q: What is your favorite class?
   你最喜欢上什么课?
   你最喜歡上甚麼課?
   A: 我最喜欢上_____课。
   A: 我最喜歡上_____課。

4. Q: Which class do you think the hardest?
　　　你觉得哪门课最难?
　　　你覺得哪門課最難?
　　A:我觉得_____课最难。
　　A:我覺得_____課最難。

NCC Step 5　Listening Comprehension Test

Instruction: Based on the paragraph/dialogue you've heard, answer the following T/F questions. Each piece will be read twice.

Paragraph:

　　小王从北京来加州大学洛杉矶分校学习美国历史。她星期一、三、五上午从十点到十点五十分都有课。她每天下午都没有课。她常去图书馆借书,也常在那儿跟朋友一起做功课。晚上她在宿舍看看书;有时候也听听录音。

　　小王從北京來加州大學洛杉磯分校學習美國歷史。她星期一、三、五上午從十點到十點五十分都有課。她每天下午都沒有課。她常去圖書館借書,也常在那兒跟朋友一起做功課。晚上她在宿舍看看書;有時候也聽聽錄音。

Dialogue:

A:小王,你这个学期都上些什么课?
A:小王,你這個學期都上些甚麼課?
B:我上物理、化学、英国文学和体育。
B:我上物理、化學、英國文學和體育。
A:你觉得哪门课最有意思?
A:你覺得哪門課最有意思?
B:文学课最有意思,可是也最难。
B:文學課最有意思,可是也最難。
A:谁是你的老师?
A:誰是你的老師?
B:我的老师是李安娜教授。
B:我的老師是李安娜教授。
A:她怎么样?
A:她怎麼樣?
B:她是从英国来的。她英文说得又清楚又漂亮,课也教得非常好。每个人喜欢上她的课。
B:她是從英國來的。她英文說得又清楚又漂亮,課也教得非常好。每個人喜歡上她的課。

Keys:
　　Paragraph: 1.T　2.F　3.T　4.T　5.T
　　Dialogue: 1.F　2.T　3.F　4.F　5.T